SETTLE TO CARLISLE

A BEAUTIFUL JOURNEY NORTH

ANTHONY LAMBERT

PARRAGON

First published in Great Britain in 1997 by

Parragon
Unit 13–17
Avonbridge Trading Estate
Atlantic Road
Avonmouth
Bristol BS11 9QD

ISBN: 0-7525-2348-1

Conceived, designed and produced by Haldane Mason, London

Acknowledgements
Art Director: Ron Samuels
Editor: Charles Dixon-Spain
Designers: Errol Campbell/Zoë Mellors
Illustrator: Claire Littlejohn
Indexer: Ian D. Crane
Picture Research: Charles Dixon-Spain

Colour reproduction by
Regent Publishing Services, Hong Kong

Printed in Hong Kong

Picture Acknowledgements
Ken Groundwater 17 (left), 22; **Hulton Picture Library** 64; **Gavin W. Morrison** 2, 5, 11, 17 (right), 18, 19, 21, 23, 28, 35, 43, 46, 48, 49 (bttm), 52, 53, 54, 60, 68, 75, 80, 81, 83, 93; **National Railway Museum, York (Science & Society Picture Library)** 8, 9 (left), 12, 14, 16, 24, 25, 26 (all), 31, 33, 34; **Dr. Les Nixon** 1, 9 (right), 27, 30, 32, 36, 42, 44, 51, 55, 58, 59, 62, 63, 65, 66, 69, 70, 74, 81 (bttm), 82, 85, 87, 88, 94; **Railfoto/Hugh Ballantyne** 15, 40, 50, 72, 73, 80, 92; **Peter J. Robinson** 29, 76, 91, 94; **David C. Rodgers** 7, 38, 41, 45, 56, 61, 77, 78, 84.

Every effort has been made to trace the copyright holders and we apologize in advance for any unintentional errors or omissions. We would be pleased to insert the appropriate acknowledgement in any subsequent edition of this publication.

Please note: Stations currently in use are given in **bold** when first mentioned in the text.

Page 1: *Northbound excursion, pulled by K1 class No. 2005, labours up the Long Drag near Selside.*
Page 2/3: *Crossing Dandry Mire with the Duchess of Hamilton.*

Contents

Introduction

No railway line in England has so captured the public imagination as the Settle & Carlisle railway (otherwise known as the S&C). It was well known before the closure threat of the 1980s and the effective campaign to save it, but the publicity these generated made the 72¹/₂ mile route the subject of national news. The ironic result has been that more passengers use the railway today than at almost any time in its history. The reasons are obvious: the story of its genesis and construction encapsulates many of the most absurd and heroic themes of Victorian railway history, and the landscapes through which it passes are simply unrivalled for beauty and sheer grandeur by any other line in the country.

Almost from the first mile of the S&C line, which begins at Settle Junction, the railway is in the Yorkshire Dales National Park and remains so for about the first 25 miles. Climbing relentlessly through Ribblesdale and skirting the upper reaches of Dentdale and Garsdale to reach what passes for a plateau in this country, between Blea Moor and Ais Gill, the line drops down the Eden Valley to reach the great railway junction of Carlisle. It passes through landscapes that hold the eye of the most blasé traveller, and could equally well have been promoted by the advertising slogan that British Rail applied to the West Highland railway in Scotland – 'A line for all seasons'. It is the kind of railway that should be experienced at different times of the year, the quality of light in such landscapes changing dramatically their atmosphere. Between Horton-in-Ribblesdale and Kirkby Stephen, Yorkshire's 'Three Peaks' – Ingleborough, Penyghent and Whernside – are in view, giving to the railway a scale that is enjoyed by few railways in Britain. As early as 1908, when marketing was still in its infancy, the Midland tried to attract hikers to the S&C and put up Ordnance Survey maps in the stations.

Yet this magnificent stretch of railway should never have been built. The story behind its construction is involved but fascinating, since it illustrates well the mentality of Parliamentarians in their dealings with railways, and the unfortunate consequences that could ensue. But before looking at the origins of the Settle & Carlisle, it is necessary to look at the great railway company that brought it into being, the Midland.

Opposite: For generations, photographers of the S&C have regarded the landscape around Ais Gill as one of the best places to record the final slog up to the summit from either direction, but particularly trains from the north, enabling the dramatic outline of Wild Boar Fell to form a backdrop. Here LNER A3 Pacific No. 4472 Flying Scotsman struggles up the last stretch to the 356 m (1,169 ft) summit with a return special to Preston on 16 May 1992.

The Midland Railway

The Midland became a splendid railway, but its origins were local and modest. One of its constituents, the Midland Counties, was founded at a meeting of local coal-owners in a pub in Eastwood, round a few corners from D.H. Lawrence's birthplace. Goods traffic, and especially coal, was the raison d'être.

The Midland was incorporated in 1844 by the amalgamation of three companies that operated in the Midlands area – the Midland Counties, the North Midland and the Birmingham & Derby Junction. Masterminded by George Hudson, whose 'Railway King' epithet belied the sharp practice that proved his eventual downfall, the merger produced the largest railway under single management in Britain.

The subsequent history of the Midland is dominated by its struggle to become a national, rather than regional, railway. This was achieved by a combination of takeovers and construction. For example, it reached Bristol by taking over the Birmingham & Gloucester and the Bristol & Gloucester railways in 1846. By building new lines it gained access to such cities as Lincoln and Peterborough in 1846, Manchester in 1867 and London in 1868, the last entailing construction of the costly line from Bedford to St. Pancras with its magnificent train shed, station and hotel. The Midland became particularly adept at forming alliances with other companies, often formalized in joint ownership of a section of railway. Amongst the more important of its arrangements, it became a partner in the Cheshire Lines Committee, thereby reaching Liverpool; the Somerset & Dorset to reach Bournemouth; and the Midland & Great Northern to tap the holiday traffic to the north Norfolk resorts and East Anglia generally. The Midland had a stake in Scotland, being a partner in the Portpatrick & Wigtownshire Joint Railways and in the company that built the Forth Bridge. It even reached the Atlantic by the acquisition of two railways in Ireland in 1903 and 1905. Finally it acquired a major slice of the London commuter traffic through its purchase of the London, Tilbury & Southend Railway in 1912. So from its early days, the Midland had ambitious goals.

In this, it was no different from other entrepreneurial railway managements of the time, but it was much more successful than most. Having risen in only a couple of decades from meetings in the back rooms of pubs to become some of the largest joint-stock enterprises anywhere in the world, the Midland, like the other larger railway companies, had an understandable optimism and belief in its ability to overcome difficulties. As Alexander Frater wrote of the two men who did most to being the S&C into being, 'Allport and Crossley were messianic Victorian visionaries who, having voted God on to the Midland board years before, felt able to tackle the trickiest problems with equilibrium.'

George Hudson was the architect behind the formation of the Midland Railway, before his dubious business practices led to his ignominious downfall.

The Midland had also become a railway of quality: its resources and profitability enabled it to construct well-designed stations using good materials, and it was renowned for the standard of upholstery and finish of its carriages. The Midland's development of comfort in its carriages placed it in the vanguard of British railway companies, especially in its concern for third-class passengers. As the Midland's great General Manager Sir James Allport said as he neared retirement, 'If there is one part of my public life on which I look back with more satisfaction than on anything else, it is with reference to the boon we conferred on third-class passengers.' However, the adoption of the beautiful crimson lake livery known as 'Midland red' with which it adorned both locomotives and carriages from 1883 was the result of an attempt to find a less fugitive and economic colour than the previous green livery for locomotives.

The characteristics evident from this resumé – determination, national aspirations and a commitment to quality – were brought to bear on one of the major difficulties that faced the Midland in the 1860s, the unacceptable delays to which its Scottish traffic was subjected.

Right: The Gothic Midland Hotel at St. Pancras, designed by Sir Gilbert Scott, has become one of London's most valued landmarks, appropriately listed Grade I. Below: William Barlow's magnificent train shed at St. Pancras has the highest arched roof of any station in Europe.

Origins

The Midland had already grown tired of an irksome dependence on other railways for forwarding its traffic to major destinations. Until the opening of a new line from Leicester to Hitchin in 1857, the Midland had relied on the London & North Western Railway (LNWR) for its London traffic, which it handed over at Rugby. Overcrowding on the West Coast main line inevitably meant that the LNWR was given priority. From the opening of the railway to Hitchin, the Midland transferred London traffic to the Great Northern Railway (GNR) which owned the railway into King's Cross. It also marked a change in allegiances for the Midland, ending its southern reliance on the LNWR and forging a closer link with the GNR.

The introduction of through Midland services into King's Cross in 1858 was a short-lived improvement; by 1862 the situation between Hitchin and King's Cross was so bad that 3,400 Midland trains were delayed that year, and in June and July the congestion had reduced both companies' traffic to chaos. The Midland determined on its own line into London. The treatment of the Midland's traffic with Scotland was little different. It was again dependent on the LNWR, handing over passengers and goods traffic at an obscure end-on junction named Ingleton. This arrangement had existed since 1861, when the Lancaster & Carlisle Railway (LCR) opened its line to Ingleton from a junction with the West Coast main line at Low Gill. The Lancaster & Carlisle directors had secured in 1859 very favourable terms for a 999-year lease to the LNWR. So the Midland was again beholden to the LNWR, which did little to smooth the operation of the Midland's traffic: stories of long waits for connections at Tebay and goods traffic taking an age to reach Carlisle fuelled the Midland's desire for a route of its own to Scotland, and it began to talk of the idea.

Because of the onerous terms of its lease of the LCR, and doubtless worried at the thought of a third main line to Scotland, the LNWR proposed in 1864 the idea of a joint lease of the LCR with the Midland. This would have given an equal voice in the handling of traffic over the line, and overcome the Midland's objections to the current position. Had these negotiations succeeded, the S&C would probably not have been built, but they foundered over the LNWR's insistence that it should have the power to regulate Midland rates on traffic to Carlisle. A less insuperable stumbling block was the LNWR's proposal that the LCR rent should be split equally between the two; this would have been very much in the LNWR's favour, since it would probably have had a much heavier traffic over the route than would ever have been built up by the Midland.

Meanwhile, north of the border, a new railway had been built that would have a bearing on the S&C. In the summer of 1862, the North British Railway completed its Waverley route from Edinburgh to Carlisle; since it was in competition with the Caledonian Railway (CR), which had a very close relationship with the LNWR, the North British was always playing second fiddle when it came to connections at Carlisle. Consequently it welcomed the prospect of a new main line from the south and a partnership with its operator.

In 1865 a Bill was put before Parliament that the Midland was to modify and re-present in the following year as the Bill for the S&C. The North of England Union Railway was for a line from a junction with the Skipton–Lancaster line south of Settle to Hawes and along Wensleydale to Leyburn on the North Eastern Railway. Without Midland intervention it would have died the death of so many hopelessly unrealistic schemes hatched in one of the two 'Railway Manias'. Such a line would never have attracted enough local traffic to make a commercial return, but the Midland saw it as an ideal vehicle for its main line to Scotland.

In August 1865 John Crossley, the Midland's Engineer, was instructed to survey the route. The possibility of North Eastern Railway opposition was nullified by the Midland truncating its eastern aspirations at Hawes. However, some Midland shareholders were not in favour of the expenditure of an estimated £1.65 million on the new line, and said so at meetings. One prescient shareholder suggested that the cost would be nearer £3 million; had his

Opposite: One of the rebuilt Royal Scot 4-6-0s allocated to Leeds Holbeck for Anglo-Scottish expresses, No. 46113 Cameronia prepares to leave the shed on 27 June 1961 to work the down 'Waverley'. The locomotive was built in 1927, rebuilt in May 1949 and withdrawn in December 1962.

warning been taken seriously, it is unlikely that shareholders would have voted for the S&C.

During the summer of 1866 a House of Commons committee heard evidence on the Midland Railway (Settle to Carlisle) Bill. Business interests from Carlisle told tales of woe about the difficulty of sending traffic through Ingleton to destinations in the Midlands, and support was given by the Glasgow & South Western, North British and Lancashire & Yorkshire railways, all frustrated in some degree by the LNWR's handling of their traffic at Carlisle or over the West Coast line. The Commons and Lords committees found in the Midland's favour and the Bill was given the Royal Assent on 16 July 1866, allowing five years for the railway's construction.

Although preparatory work for construction was begun by Crossley, it was to be three years before the Midland really had the bit between its teeth. Firstly, a reduction in the Midland dividend did not dispose shareholders favourably either to a proposed amalgamation with the Glasgow & South Western Railway or the amount of money that the Midland was committed to laying out on a range of new works – estimated at £5 million. The two issues became bound up, and a group of Midland shareholders approached the LNWR to try to negotiate a new agreement for use of the LCR. Those trying to stop the S&C proceeding were fearful of the impact the costs would have on their dividends – and perhaps on those of the LNWR, since many held shares in both companies. In the event, the Lords rejected the amalgamation Bill.

The deteriorating economic position in the country at large towards the end of 1867 prompted the Midland board to suspend further work and land purchase for the S&C. The tide of opposition from shareholders was such that the Midland board felt it had no option but to agree to cooperate with a committee of consultation to look at ways of reducing or limiting the impact of outstanding new works. A dialogue between the committee and the LNWR suggested that the prospect of the S&C had concentrated the mind of the North Western board at Euston: much more conciliatory ideas were put forward to meet the Midland's

Surmounted by the Wyvern of Mercia, the heraldic device of the Midland included the arms of Bristol, Derby, Leeds, Leicester and Lincoln, supported by a dolphin and a salamander.

needs over the LCR and so more formal talks between the Midland and the LNWR were held in July and August of 1868 to see if some accommodation could be reached.

Negotiations were sufficiently favourable for the Midland directors to consider dropping the S&C, but they faced a dilemma. To cancel the S&C an abandonment Bill would have to be put before Parliament, but the outcome would not be known until May 1869. On the other hand, two years of the S&C Bill had already elapsed without any material work having been done, and on 16 July 1869 the Midland's powers for the compulsory purchase of land would lapse, necessitating an extension of powers. How could the Midland apply for a Bill to abandon the S&C at the same time as it sought an extension of powers to build it?

The only course was to put the quandary openly before the LNWR board, which could see that the Midland had little option but to present both Bills. By November 1868 agreement between the two railways for the Midland's use of the LCR had been reached, and the LNWR would support the S&C abandonment Bill.

The alliances that had debated the merits of the original S&C Bill were now turned on their heads. The Midland's erstwhile supporters now became staunch opponents of the abandonment Bill. The pros and cons of cancelling the S&C were closely argued before a House of Commons committee in April 1869, and it is hard to find fault with the arguments put forward by the Midland's counsel, but the opposition mounted a strong case that their traffic would not be helped by joint working of the LCR in the way that it would by construction of the S&C. The fervent determination of Parliament to do all in its power to resist anything that smacked of monopoly status, and to stimulate competition irrespective of possible waste, informed many of the decisions it took about railways in the Victorian era. And so it was with the S&C abandonment Bill. After seven days of hearings, the committee found the preamble of the Bill not proven. The Midland was committed to building the S&C.

LMS Jubilee class 4-6-0 No. 45562 Alberta heads the up (southbound) Waverley at Ais Gill in about 1960. These were the last express engines to operate the S&C in BR days.

Construction

The sheer scale of the task facing the engineer charged with building the S&C, John Sidney Crossley, must have been daunting, even for a man of his experience. It is a pity that there is no diary of the epic walk that Crossley and Sir James Allport made of the route when the idea of the S&C was still in its infancy; it would be fascinating to know the impressions of the two men as they tramped across 'that terrible place, Blea Moor', as Sir James later recounted.

Although there were no complex bridges to build, such as those over the Tamar estuary at Saltash or across the Menai Strait, the number of structures was formidable: 85 overbridges, 150 underbridges, 25 viaducts with 168 openings and 13 tunnels. As a farmer said, with pardonable exaggeration, to the two pioneers during their walk: 'I declare to you there is not a level piece of ground big enough to build a house upon all the way between Settle and Carlisle.' Moreover the terrain was harsh and almost certain to provide some unpleasant surprises, which proved to be the case, compelling more costly and time-consuming solutions where no problem had been anticipated: embankments turned into viaducts, cuttings into tunnels.

Right: The imposing profile of Ribblehead Viaduct with a Carlisle-bound train.
Below: The arches of Ribblehead Viaduct, which required extensive work in the 1990s to remedy the effects of water working into the stonework and then freezing.

J. C. Bourne's depiction of Kilsby Tunnel on the London & Birmingham line shows the sort of desperate conditions the navvies of the S&C worked in.

The scale of the works was a reflection of the Midland's determination to produce a line for the express speeds of the day. By stipulating a maximum gradient of 1 in 100, the Midland denied itself the freedom to take full advantage of the contours of the hills as the North of England Union Railway (NEUR) had done in its plans for a railway from Settle to Hawes. When the Midland took over the project, it had to discard most of the route surveyed, since the NEUR was never intended to be more than a relatively slow, branch line. To maintain the capability of high speed running, the Midland was forced into much heavier engineering works. A by-product of the priority given to through, rather than intermediate traffic, is the distance that separates most of the stations from the towns or villages they were built to serve. The S&C was also constructed with little thought of economy in the engineering and architectural standards that were set; there was never a sense that the Midland was going to skimp on this railway simply because it had been forced into building it against its will.

In as much as it can be said that a railway was principally the work of one man, the S&C owed more to Crossley than anyone else. Crossley was the Midland's Engineer from 1857 to 1878. Orphaned at the age of two in 1815, he had clearly shown early promise, becoming engineer of the Leicester Navigation Canal at the age of 20. He first became involved with what became a constituent part of the Midland in 1832 when he carried out surveying work on the Leicester & Swannington Railway. The rest of his life was spent surveying and supervising the construction of hundreds of miles of the Midland, culminating with the S&C.

The line was scheduled for completion in just under four years, ready for opening in the summer of 1873. In fact it was another two years before the first goods train traversed the line and the opening to passengers did not take place until 1 May 1876. The works were divided into four contracts: No. 1, 17 miles from Settle Junction to Dent Head; No. 2, 17 miles on to Smardale; No. 3 14^1/$_2$ miles to New Biggin; and No. 4, the remaining 24 miles to Petteril Bridge.

Construction began in November 1869 with that very Victorian occasion, the cutting of the first sod, in the grounds of Anley House near Settle. Such events were usually attended by local worthies, as well as officials, and carried out with a ceremonial silver spade and beautifully crafted wheelbarrow.

Naturally a start was made on those works that were expected to take the longest; by March 1870 the shafts for Blea Moor Tunnel were well under way,

Though rudimentary, the facilities of a gangers' hut on the S&C would have been very welcome in winter, when the efficient stove could create quite a heat.

The plaque in the church at Settle which commemorates those killed and injured during construction of the S&C. The plaque was paid for by the MR and navvies.

and a number of boreholes sunk to determine the location of rock for viaduct foundations. However, it was quickly evident that work on No. 1 contract was slipping behind schedule, a position that was to worsen: the contractor had to ask the Midland for a loan, which it provided, but by October 1871 things had reached the point at which the Midland felt compelled to cancel the contract and assume direct responsibility for the work. This added significantly to the burden on Crossley. Finding enough navvies to progress the works at an adequate pace was another perennial problem. The appalling weather and

physical conditions ate away at the men's morale, and all but the most determined quit after months rather than years; on No. 2 contract there was a 73% turnover of navvies in a single month. Although there were up to 7,000 navvies at work at any one time, hundreds of thousands of men experienced the hardships of an S&C navvy's life. In common with most railway construction, navvies were lured away during harvest time, especially in the Eden Valley area, where their help in the fields was most needed. Rates of pay were good for the times. They had to be to attract men to work in such atrocious conditions, but many men

Above: LMS 4F 0-6-0 No. 44276 with large snowplough at Skipton shed in 1965.
Opposite: LNER A3 Pacific No. 4472 Flying Scotsman near Ais Gill summit.

who were on piece rates decided that by about 15.00 they had earned enough for the day and downed tools. Those who were paid by the day put in the required number of hours but, as Crossley euphemistically put it, 'do not work to hurt themselves.'

Another difficulty was the transport of equipment, materials and supplies to such a remote area, in which there were few roads, and most were little more than farm tracks or drove roads. The component parts of stationary steam winding engines for the top of tunnel shafts had to be manhandled across boggy ground and up steep slopes. Once in place they had to be assembled in the open, with minimal facilities, and were then used to haul further supplies up the slopes. In contrast to railway construction a few decades earlier, the S&C was able to benefit from improved mechanisation in such equipment as drills and from safer materials, particularly dynamite rather than gun-cotton.

However, pick and shovel were still to the fore; by the time the Great Central main line to London came to be built in the final decade of the century, mechanical excavators were doing most of the work.

Nor were the soil conditions conducive to easy work. For much of the southern section the builders had to contend with boulder clay, which could change its nature from one day to the next. As Crossley recounted to the early historian of the Midland, Frederick Williams, 'I have known the men blast the boulder-clay like rock, and within a few hours to have to ladle out the same stuff from the same spot like soup in buckets. Or a man strikes a blow with his pick at what he thinks is clay, but there is a great boulder underneath almost as hard as iron, and the man's wrists, arms, and body are so shaken by the shock, that, disgusted, he flings down his tools, asks for his money, and is off.'

Conditions were inevitably worsened by the amount of rain that can lash the Dales, turning already difficult ground into quagmires. No. 2 contract was particularly affected by rain: cartwheels had to be replaced by massive rollers to prevent them sinking into the glutinous mud that the clay had become, horses sank up to their bellies and even dragging a telegraph pole along might require the exertions of four horses. Crossley was tried by some exceptionally bad weather: in 1872, for example, 152 cm (60 in) of rain fell at Kirkby Stephen instead of the average 94 cm (37 in).

Rain was not the only trial. Frost would halt masonry work for days and turn previously sticky clay as hard as concrete. Only the tunnellers could remain at work in such conditions: hundreds of feet below the surface of the moor, navvies laboured for 12-hour shifts in a stygian gloom, relieved only by the feeble light of candles. Williams went through the workings and thought them 'a picture fit for Rembrandt', though Wright of Derby might have been a more apposite choice.

Crossley had underestimated the impact the weather would have on the progress of the works. His reports to the Midland construction committee are full of frustration at the way inclement conditions not only impeded work, but encouraged those navvies on piece rates to leave altogether because they could not work enough hours to amass a decent wage.

Another factor which deterred navvies from staying long on the S&C was the high incidence of deaths and injuries: of those based at Batty Moss camp near Ribblehead alone, about a hundred died from all causes during construction. There was also the fear of smallpox – a severe outbreak at Ribblehead in 1871 was the principal cause behind the need to expand the graveyard at nearby Chapel-le-Dale, and it also broke out in Settle in 1871–2, prompting the Midland to give £100 to the town's smallpox hospital. Fighting,

which was a way of life in the camps, caused a number of fatalities. On Sundays, when no work was done, bare-knuckle fights would be held for the title of camp champion, who might be pitted against a professional fighter brought in for the spectacle.

Though the navvies were undoubtedly rough and sometimes violent, there was another side to their behaviour. When the missionary for the 17 miles between Settle and Denthead, James Tiplady, left after two years' work in 1872, he was given a silver cruet and an illuminated address by the inhabitants of the camp at Ribblehead in appreciation of his efforts. He had described his flock as being 'with few exceptions a good-hearted, generously disposed class. The greatest enemy I have to contend with is strong drink. If this could be removed, a great boon would be conferred, not only upon the Missionary, but upon all who have anything to do with railway work.'

Goods trains began operating over the line in early August 1875 (there is some doubt over the precise date), and it opened to passenger trains without fuss or ceremony on 1 May 1876. The previous month the construction committee had toured the line in a cattle truck fitted out with wooden benches so that the party could enjoy a clear view. The combination of this unusual mode of travel with the grandeur of the landscapes induced an extravagant description from the *Sheffield & Rotherham Independent* reporter: 'There, in appropriate wrappings and in close-fitting caps, with nothing to obstruct their view of the line – they were enabled to appreciate the glories of land and sky, the ranges of mighty mountains, intersected by wild gorges or divided by lovely valleys. . . .' The correspondent went on to suggest that such vehicles might become a permanent option for hardier travellers, an idea that was certainly adopted in Switzerland and the United States.

In common with most civil engineering works on such a scale, the costs were underestimated: the line cost £3.8 million rather than the anticipated £2.2 million. Crossley cannot be blamed for much of the overspend. It was his and the Midland's misfortune that construction of the S&C should coincide with a period of exceptional inflation. The various causes behind several years of increases in prices and wages included, in 1866, the second Railway Mania and the collapse of the discount house Overend, Gurney & Co (which caused the worst panic in the city since 1825) and the Franco-Prussian War of 1870–1. The consequence was increases in some wages of up to 100 % within a year and a tripling in the price of coal between 1870 and 1876.

Class 47 No. 47104 crosses Arten Gill Viaduct with a Cleethorpes-Carlisle special. In recent years locomotives have been seen only on freight and diversions.

Architecture

Most of the station buildings on the S&C were based on a standard design evolved by Crossley which has been called 'Midland Gothic', though the architect of the S&C buildings was I. H. Sanders.

There were three levels of provision according to the anticipated traffic. A common feature of the two smaller categories was a central section housing a waiting area protected by a wood- or iron-framed screen, flanked by two gabled pavilions. The more important stations of Appleby and Settle had three pavilions, and Garsdale, Crosby Garrett and Culgaith had differently designed buildings. Many of the stations had low platforms, requiring portable wooden steps to assist some passengers.

Goods sheds were as solidly built as the stations, their size naturally determined by the expectations for traffic, ranging from a two-wagon shed at Armathwaite to five-wagon sheds at Settle, Kirkby Stephen and Appleby.

Materials were extracted locally to reduce transport costs, limestone being used in upper Ribblesdale, gritstone at Dent and Garsdale, and sandstone through the Eden Valley.

A measure of the railway's architectural and historic importance was the decision in 1991 by North Yorkshire County Council to designate the whole line within the Yorkshire Dales National Park as a conservation area. This includes lineside structures, the land on which Batty Moss shanty town once stood and even the heaps of spoil excavated from Blea Moor Tunnel. It is believed to be the first time that a working railway has been declared a linear conservation area.

The Friends of the Settle–Carlisle Line have also done much to retain the surviving buildings that lend such character to a journey over the line.

Right: Some of the decorative spandrels of the station roof at Hellifield are adorned with the Midland wyvern. For years under threat of demolition, the station has been given a new lease of life thanks to the imaginative co-operation of a range of organizations.
Opposite: Hellifield, like many a country junction, has lost its importance, but it may become a junction again if services from Blackburn are extended north.

Passenger Services

At first trains were formed of MR stock, but the hire charges levied by the MR on the North British and Glasgow & South Western railways led to the formation of Midland Scotch Joint Stock - carriages and vans that were owned by all three companies and initialled MSJS on their sides. Reorganization at the turn of the century led to a separation of Glasgow and Edinburgh service carriages, the former becoming M&GSW property only, the latter M&NB.

There were six S&C trains to and from St. Pancras, of which two were expresses, referred to as the Scotch expresses, two semi-fasts and a morning and afternoon all-stations stopping train. Competition with the West Coast route was rather unequal, since the LNWR line to Carlisle was almost an hour quicker, partly thanks to easier grades over most of a distance 10 miles shorter than the MR route. To counteract the LNWR's advantage of speed, the MR included on one train each way an American Pullman car, a huge bogie vehicle with open saloon accommodation;

One of the opulent Midland first-class dining-cars, depicted in an official card.

the day train carried a drawing-room car while the night train had a sleeping car.

A half-hour stop at Normanton was required on the northbound daytime Scotch express to allow passengers to have lunch; the first dining car in Britain had yet to be introduced, in 1879, and it was not until 1892 that the MR had its first dining carriages. The night train had a stop of 15 minutes at Leeds for refreshments and engine change. To save time, orders for lunch were taken on the train and telegraphed from Leicester to Normanton (a similar practice still obtains on many trains in India). The challenge of the lunch stop must have been daunting for passengers: as the *Railway News* reported, 'A dinner of five courses, with dessert, and no fees to waiters, is prepared at Normanton, and half-an-hour is allowed for the discussion and disposal of the good things so liberally provided.' Since there were no lavatories in Midland stock running over the S&C, time would also have to be found for a visit to the doubtlessly hard-pressed facilities in the station unless, as Peter Baughan put it, they had 'an abundance of private patience.'

By the early years of the twentieth century there were five day trains to Scotland from St. Pancras, three to Glasgow and two to Edinburgh, supplemented by three overnight trains: one to Stranraer Harbour, one that served Glasgow and Edinburgh, and a later train to Glasgow only. In the summer months there was also an overnight train to Inverness, in 1905 leaving St. Pancras at midnight and reaching the Highland capital at 07.50. Facilities on expresses had improved immeasurably: lavatories in carriages could be taken for granted; dining-cars were provided on many trains; even sets of chess and draughts could be obtained from conductors on Scotch expresses.

In 1927, the principal Scottish trains from St. Pancras were named the 'Thames–Clyde Express' (to Glasgow) and the 'Thames–Forth Express'

Royal Scot class 4-6-0 No. 46145 The Duke of Wellington's Regt. (West Riding) waits to leave Leeds with the 'Thames-Clyde Express', the S&C's longest-used express name.

(to Edinburgh), the latter being renamed 'the Waverley' after the war. 'The Waverley' came to an end with the short-sighted closure in January 1969 of the former North British Railway main line between Carlisle and Edinburgh, which had acquired the name 'the Waverley route'.

During both world wars, in common with all parts of the railway system, traffic levels increased dramatically. For example, in a 25-hour period in August 1914, no fewer than 67 special trains of naval and military personnel travelled over the S&C. None the less, the brunt of extra wartime traffic was borne by the West Coast main line.

In 1922 about 150 railways were amalgamated into four large companies, the Midland becoming part of the London, Midland & Scottish Railway. The main effect on S&C services was a reduction in the number of through carriages on the expresses that used the line. The range of options for passengers out of St. Pancras was reduced, the West Coast main line carrying the majority of the LMS Anglo-Scottish services.

Schoolchildren used the S&C intensively, local trains taking pupils from smaller villages to district centres such as Appleby and Settle. But even in the Midland days, when there was little competition from buses or cars, the local trains made little money for the railway. The first station to be closed to passengers was Scotby, in 1942, but more followed in the early 1950s. As plans for electrification of the West Coast main line developed, it became evident that British Railways wished to retain only the two ends of the S&C to serve mineral workings, closing the central section entirely. A proposal to withdraw passenger services from all remaining stations except Settle and Appleby was turned down by the Minister of Transport in 1964. In April 1966, diesel-multiple-unit paytrains were introduced to allow station staff to be reduced, but closure of local services apart from Settle and Appleby stations gained ministerial approval and took place from 5 May 1970. This left only three express trains a day, one of them overnight.

Through passenger trains were largely diverted on to the West Coast main line from May 1982, after which there were only two trains a day between Leeds and Carlisle.

Above: A Midland first-class dining-car with buttoned, leather upholstery and clerestory roof. The lighting was by gas, which was responsible for the fire in the Hawes Junction disaster of 1910. Right: A third-class dining-car, showing prints above the seats and the ornate brass bottle holders.

THE LAKE DISTRICT FOR HOLIDAYS
LONDON MIDLAND AND SCOTTISH RAILWAY

LMS Duchess Pacific No. 46229 Duchess of Hamilton heads north from Garsdale, probably after stopping for water.

Goods Services

The individual sources of goods traffic are covered in the following sections, but a few general points are worth making. The sparsely populated countryside served by the S&C made it inevitable that revenue from the carriage of general merchandise to and from S&C stations would never thrill the commercial manager, but this was somewhat compensated for by substantial volumes of livestock traffic, until reduced by lorry competition, and by mineral traffic from quarries and works served by the railway.

So much traffic was generated by some of the sheep and cattle sales at stations such as Appleby and Lazonby that extra staff had to be sent to cope, usually relief porters from other stations along the line. Each station had a hut containing sawdust for cattle wagons, which were washed out and disinfected at Hellifield. Between 1906 and 1915, an average of about 9,000 wagonloads of livestock a year were generated by S&C stations.

Some passenger and goods traffic overlapped: for many years the last northbound stopping train had two large vans for milk churns; each bore the name of the farm on a brass plate and was arranged in order for offloading at the nearest station.

The majority of goods trains over the S&C were, of course, through trains. A measure of the volume is given by the transfer during June 1876 of 9,403 wagons between the Midland and the GSWR/NBR at Carlisle. Given the modest power of steam locomotives at the time, this amounted to a substantial number of trains. The S&C was an important freight artery for almost 110 years, especially during the wars when there would be a goods train in almost every one of the 30–35 block sections between signal boxes. As late as March 1959, the S&C was chosen as the route for new Condor non-stop container service which left Hendon, in London, at 19.23 and arrived in Glasgow at 05.20. Even when the Beeching report of 1963 raised a question mark over the whole future of the line, it was carrying 100,000 tons of freight a week.

The S&C was of great value for diverted freight services while wires were being put up along the West Coast main line, and it continued to be so after electrification because all catch points were removed at the same time. This meant that unfitted (without operative brakes on all wagons) freights had to use the S&C. However, the elimination of vacuum-braked wagons in favour of fully air-braked freight trains meant that this benefit of the S&C was eliminated. The

An LMS Crab 2-6-0 heads south with a freight near Ais Gill summit – the fireman's labour is very nearly over.

A Loadhaul-liveried Class 60 No. 60007 crosses Ais Gill Viaduct southbound with empty containers from Kirkby Thore to Drax power station. In the background is the footbridge known as Hangman's Bridge, supposedly after a suicide.

last through freight ran in May 1983, leaving only a few short-lived mineral flows from Ribblehead and Ministry of Defence traffic to Warcop on the truncated NER Eden Valley line. Freight returned in 1993 when Trainload Freight (TLF) began to fulfil a ten-year contract to move desulphogypsum from Drax to Kirkby Thore north of Appleby. TLF's regional successor, Transrail, routed regular trains of coal containers from Selby to the Highlands over the S&C from 12 August 1995, and Transrail's new owner, English, Welsh & Scottish Railway, is pursuing new sources of traffic on the line.

Locomotives

When the S&C opened, the 300 miles between St. Pancras and Carlisle was beyond the capacity of any locomotives, so a change of motive power was required at Leicester, Normanton and Skipton; the night trains changed engines at Leeds instead of both Skipton and Normanton. So efficient was this operation that it required just four minutes.

Throughout its 79 years, the Midland had what was called 'a small engine policy': rather than building large locomotives, the company preferred engines that were adequate for running fast with light trains. If necessary, a pilot engine would be provided for heavier trains or over steep gradients such as those on the S&C. The Midland never had anything larger than a 4-4-0 – most of the larger pre-grouping companies had built 4-4-2s or 4-6-0s – though Deeley did design a compound 4-6-0 which was rejected by the Midland board.

The first S&C passenger trains were hauled by various classes of 2-4-0s, especially Kirtley's 800 class, while goods trains were hauled by 0-6-0s, as they were throughout the Midland era. On passenger trains the 2-4-0s were joined by the first 4-4-0s, Carlisle receiving its first 4-4-0 in 1882–3 and Skipton as late as 1894. The first compound 4-4-0 was tested over the S&C in 1902, No. 2631 running the 76.7 miles from Carlisle to Settle in just 81 minutes. The following year they were introduced on some expresses. The later compounds were to prove in trials that they could eclipse the performance of ostensibly larger and more powerful engines. Compounds by no means had a monopoly of express working: 20 of Johnson's extremely handsome 60 class 4-4-0s were

The Midland's first three-cylinder compound 4-4-0, No. 2631, emerged from Derby works in 1901 with a massive 4500-gallon tender – the first watertroughs on the MR were built two years later. An indicator shield is fitted for test runs.

LMS 4-4-0 Class 4 Compound No. 1045 and Jubilee class 4-6-0 No. 5562 Alberta on a southbound express near Ais Gill on 27 July 1939. Note the two milk tanks.

assigned to the S&C in 1901, and of Deeley's 4-4-0 classes, the ten superheated 990 class were put on to principal trains from 1907.

After the grouping, it was obviously necessary for the chief mechanical engineer of the 'Big Four' railway companies to devise a new locomotive policy. To help them do this, comparative trials were often organized to evaluate the characteristics of the locomotives they inherited and to formulate design criteria for the future. Sometimes locomotives were borrowed from 'rival' companies. Since the West Coast main line was more heavily trafficked than the S&C, the latter was an obvious choice for such tests, particularly given its challenging gradients. The first trials were held in December 1923–January 1924 between a Midland Compound 4-4-0, a Midland simple 4-4-0 and a LNWR 'Prince of Wales' 4-6-0. The Compound won hands down, although it was a more recently overhauled engine than the other two.

The Compound was challenged by a much larger LNWR Claughton 4-6-0 and by a Caledonian Pickersgill 4-4-0 in more tests the following November and December. The locomotives were in such disparate mechanical condition that one wonders why they bothered to hold the tests; little was learned from the results. However, a decision was taken to try Claughtons on the S&C, and 20 were divided between Leeds Holbeck and Carlisle Durran Hill sheds in 1927; the former LNWR section of the LMS used the opportunity to pass on examples in inferior condition and they were not popular with the crews.

During the 1930s, newly designed classes were introduced on passenger trains such as the Patriot, Jubilee and Black Five 4-6-0s, while goods trains were mostly entrusted to Fowler's Crab 2-6-0s, 0-6-0s and Black Fives. For the first time, tank engines might be seen on local trains, especially those working from the south to Hawes.

The most significant change during the Second World War was the introduction of the three-cylinder Royal Scot class 4-6-0s on passenger trains and Stanier's 8F 2-8-0s and War Department Austerity 2-8-0s on freight. After nationalization, Britannias and Clans, both Pacifics, were seen on expresses, followed in the early 1960s by some former London & North Eastern Railway A3 Pacifics which had been displaced by diesels on the East Coast main line. Riddles's 9F 2-10-0s became regular performers on the heavier freights.

Many classes of diesel operated over the route, some diverted off the West Coast main line, and the line became one of the last places to see Class 31s on passenger workings.

LMS 8F No. 48090 blasts out of Birkett tunnel. Note the initials 'MR' on the moulding at the top of the left-hand abutment.

Operation

The S&C was never going to be an easy line to operate, but it was challenges posed by appalling weather conditions that often brought out the best spirit in railwaymen. Equally the gradients that gave the line its nickname of the 'Long Drag' were a test of the skills of driver and fireman, who could expect to shovel 4–5 tons of coal in a shift when working a heavy train.

Even a descending goods train required a sure touch, since couplings had to be kept taught; the driver had to keep steam on while the guard in his brake van would have the brakes hard on, often shooting off a catherine wheel of sparks and sometimes causing the wheels and brake gear to glow red hot.

Besides snow, the wind could be a serious trial, sometimes reducing the speed of trains perceptibly when they emerged from a sheltered stretch of line into the teeth of a gale at such places as Ribblehead. The Helm Wind, heralded by long bars of white cloud over the hills with a darker band below, can blow for up to three days. It is especially fierce in late spring and autumn, and also bitterly cold, but it can also blow during the winter and cause severe drifting of snow. Massive snowploughs were kept at Carlisle and Hellifield. Attached to two or three locomotives, they would charge drifts, hitting them with such an impact that derailments could occur.

During the notoriously bad winter of early 1947, Dent was one of the worst places on the S&C line. Taken in February, this photograph shows the southbound line on the left is still blocked.

The exceptionally severe months of February/March 1947 saw some extraordinary sights on the S&C. The line was more or less closed to through traffic for much of the two months, and snow obliterated buildings and even overbridges, so deep were the drifts. One railwayman remembers helping to get wagons of hay to farmers whose animals had no food, and how animals had to be found shelter; one day, a freak shower literally caused rabbits and hares caught in fields beside the line to die in a coat of ice. Besides hundreds of railwaymen, troops and German prisoners of war were drafted into the area to assist in snow-clearing operations. Wagons would be filled with snow which would then be tipped over the sides of nearby viaducts, producing a spectacular sight when caught by the sun.

Matters became so desperate in 1947 that a Whitley jet engine was obtained and placed on a flat truck, but the snow was so compacted that it blew it off in chunks and the experiment was abandoned after clearing only 27 m (30 yd) in several hours.

A Whitley Mark II jet engine struggles in vain to clear snow on 22 February 1947 under the auspices of the Ministry of Supply's snow dispersal unit.

Salvation and Renaissance

There have been two cycles of revival on the S&C during the last three decades, but the first proved a false dawn that was followed by the closure proposal. In turn this provoked the best organized campaign in Britain against the closure of a railway. It created a national awareness of the S&C that has attracted passengers from all over Britain and further afield. But a little background to the story is necessary.

Beeching's 1963 report on *The Reshaping of British Railways* left little ground for optimism for the long-term future of the S&C. It was expected that once the West Coast main line was electrified, the S&C would soon be closed. However, experience of trying to interweave fast electric passenger trains with slower moving freight on the West Coast main line from the start of electric services in 1974 prompted a rethink about the S&C's value as a freight and diversionary route. The need to operate unfitted freights over the S&C has already been touched upon, and added to the reasons for a stay of execution. Meanwhile, some arrears of maintenance were tackled.

LMS Duchess Pacific No. 46229 Duchess of Hamilton on a photo run-past at Ribblehead. This locomotive has made some outstanding runs over the S&C.

Work in progress on the decking of Ribblehead Viaduct. The ingress of water into the spandrels, followed by freezing weather, caused cracking in the arches. The estimate of remedial work became a bone of contention between British Rail and those fighting to save the S&C from closure.

The beginning of the S&C's first renaissance came with the reopening of five stations – Horton-in-Ribblesdale, Ribblehead, Dent, Garsdale and Kirkby Stephen – for the Dales Rail services which first ran during the summer of 1975. These were intended to provide an alternative means of access to the National Park, the proportion and number of car-borne visitors being an increasing concern to the authorities of all National Parks. Buses met trains at Garsdale to extend the range of day visits. Trains ran from Leeds to Appleby, and carried 10,000 passengers in twelve days.

The success of the experiment encouraged Langwathby, Lazonby and Armathwaite to be added the following year, as well as trains from Manchester, Preston and Colne. This triumph of new partnerships between British Rail, county councils, the Countryside Commission, bus companies and the park authorities enabled the centenary of the S&C to be celebrated with some optimism. Special trains, some steam-hauled, were operated and a grand banquet held. Dales Rail services continued until the formal reopening on a permanent basis of all these stations on 14 July 1986.

In 1978 specials hauled by preserved steam locomotives were permitted to operate over the S&C on an experimental basis, leading two years later to the introduction of the triangular Cumbrian Mountain Express, which was steam hauled from Carlisle to Skipton and Skipton to Carnforth. The future for such encouraging developments was thrown into doubt by the statement in 1981 that Ribblehead needed £4.25–6m spending on it within five years or the line would have to be shut (this figure was quite rightly questioned by independent civil engineers). Simultaneously it was announced that the three remaining Nottingham–Glasgow trains would be rerouted via the Hope Valley,

Manchester and Preston. From May 1982 only two Leeds–Carlisle trains would be left.

Fears were realized in August 1983 when formal closure notices were posted. An entire book has been written about the campaign to save the S&C that took place over the next six years, culminating in a reprieve in April 1989. A major role in the fight to save the line was played by the Friends of the Settle–Carlisle Line, which had been founded in 1981 and became one of the constituent organizations of the Settle–Carlisle Joint Action Committee, along with the Railway Development Society and Transport 2000. Its work was decisively bolstered by the support of local authorities, led by Cumbria County Council, which was instrumental in forming a Joint Councils Steering Group. The campaign was also helped by the fact that the line traverses a number of political constituencies whose MPs did not relish the loss of such a high-profile and exceptional railway. Once the campaign was won, the Committee was disbanded, but the Friends has continued to play a major role in the physical improvement of the railway and its promotion. Amongst other functions, they have taken responsibility for the upkeep of station gardens: flower-beds are beautifully planted and maintained, making S&C stations some of most attractive on Britain's railways.

Ironically, British Rail's appointment of Ron Cotton as the S&C project manager with the task of closing the line proved to be a boon to the campaign against closure. A marketing man by background with the success of the Saver ticket scheme to his credit, Mr Cotton promoted the line so ably that he quadrupled the number of passengers. It was with the help of Mr Cotton that the Joint Councils acted to improve the train service and reopen the eight stations served by the Dales Rail trains on 14 July 1986. Patronage was sufficiently encouraging for the councils to pledge support of £0.5 million when asked by the Minister with responsibility for public transport how much they would be prepared to put on the table.

After three more years of chicanery and a vain attempt to find a private-sector buyer for the line, a reprieve of the S&C was announced on 11 April 1989. Arrears of maintenance have been steadily made good, including the £3 million restoration of Ribblehead Viaduct which was completed in June 1992. Today the line is carrying a healthy local traffic, especially in the summer when it helps to reduce the number of cars choking the roads of the National Park. For the sake of a country faced with the prospect of worsening vehicle pollution and congestion, it is to be hoped that a repetition of the extraordinary campaign to save England's finest stretch of railway will never again be needed, on the S&C's account or any other civilized lifeline of communities.

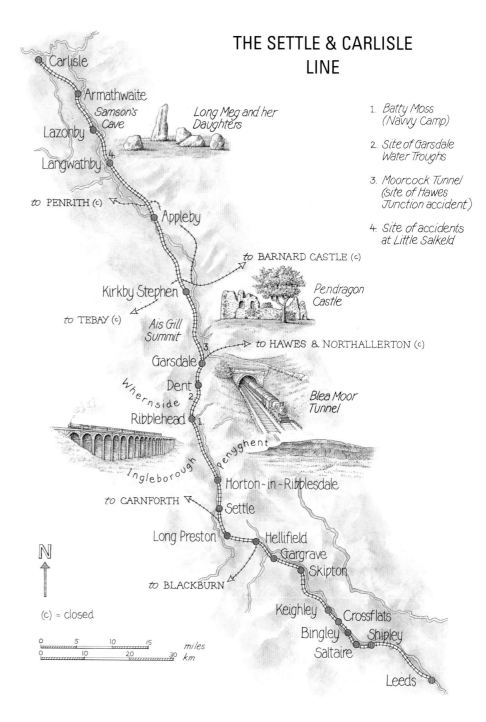

THE SETTLE & CARLISLE LINE

1. Batty Moss (Navvy Camp)

2. Site of Garsdale Water Troughs

3. Moorcock Tunnel (site of Hawes Junction accident)

4. Site of accidents at Little Salkeld

(c) = closed

Leeds–Ribblehead

The regular train service over the Settle & Carlisle begins at Leeds, sharing the line through Airedale with the electric trains that run as far as Skipton. Though the S&C does not commence until Settle Junction, it is worth mentioning a few highlights of the first 39 miles of the journey, although S&C trains stop only at Shipley and Keighley between Leeds and Skipton.

Two miles west of Leeds on the right-hand side are the remains of the Cistercian abbey at Kirkstall, where the gatehouse contains a small museum. Trains from Bradford connect at the triangular junction of Shipley, after which the next stop for local trains is **Saltaire**.

This outstanding model community was founded by the enlightened manufacturer Sir Titus Salt, who created in the 1850s 792 houses, chapels, churches, a hospital, school, park and laundry, and almshouses for the families that worked in his vast mohair and alpaca mill – the world's largest factory when it opened. Part of the six-storey mill has been converted into the 1853 Gallery which houses the largest collection of works by Bradford-born David Hockney.

Bingley is known for the impressive Five Rise Locks on the Leeds & Liverpool Canal, which opened in 1774, though trees screen the canal from the railway. However, prominent on the right of the line is Bowling Green Mill, which was built in 1871 and is now occupied by Damart.

The larger mill town of **Keighley** is junction for the Keighley & Worth Valley Railway, a largely steam-operated preserved railway that takes passengers to Haworth (for the Brontë parsonage) and Oxenhope.

Promoted as the 'Gateway to the Dales', **Skipton** is connected with several places served by the S&C through Lady Anne Clifford (1590–1676). This remarkable woman was born at the large castle, today a well-preserved medieval structure open to the public. Brought up in London and successively chatelaine of Knole in Kent and Wilton in Wiltshire, Lady Anne eventually succeeded to the northern estates that her father's will had denied her. She came north in 1649 and devoted the last 27 years of her life to rebuilding castles and building or restoring churches and almshouses over a large area.

The station at Skipton was opened on 30 April 1876, the day before the first passenger trains ran over the S&C, and has endured fewer alterations than most comparable-sized stations. Particularly attractive are the ridge-and-furrow canopies supported by decorative columns and brackets.

Although Skipton was once a junction of importance, **Hellifield** was the more significant as far as the S&C was concerned. It became a junction six years after the S&C opened, when the Lancashire & Yorkshire Railway (LYR) extended its line from Blackburn to join the Midland in 1880. From being a small village, Hellifield became a railway community, with hundreds of people employed or supported by the railway. In 1895 the MR engine shed alone employed 80 men against an allocation of 28 locomotives, and the LYR also had an engine shed. A large number of guards were based at Hellifield – in the late 1930s there were 24 goods and 8 passenger guards – and both companies had sets of sidings, dealing with 200,000 wagons a year in the period just before the First World War.

The station itself had a uniformed staff of 60 in its heyday. Until 1921 there were first- and third-class refreshment rooms employing a manageress, three waitresses, a cook, cellarman and a boy who took a basket of fruit and chocolates along the platform whenever a train called. Predictably, Burton beer was sold in the refreshment room; it was unavailable elsewhere in the district so many farmers preferred to drink at the station. W. H. Smith had a shop from 1901 until 1956.

Standing on the island platform today, it is hard to imagine such 24-hour activity – the station is now an unstaffed halt, and the engine sheds and all but a few empty sidings have disappeared. However, the Grade II listed stone buildings and elaborate canopies have been renovated, thanks to a partnership that included Railtrack, the Railway Heritage Trust and local organizations; £0.5 million has been spent on restoration work, and part of the space has been let.

LMS Pacific No. 46229 Duchess of Hamilton heads north at Stainforth with a Cumbrian Mountain Express in 1993.

Between **Gargrave** and Bell Busk, the railway crosses over the Leeds & Liverpool Canal. The Settle & Carlisle line begins 234 miles from St. Pancras at Settle Junction, where it leaves what was once the Midland's main route to Scotland through Ingleton; today the line is reduced to secondary status, carrying trains between Leeds, Lancaster and Morecambe. The junction marks the start of the taxing climb up to Blea Moor Tunnel, nearly 15 miles of an almost unbroken 1 in 100 gradient. The signal box of 1913 can be seen on the left. The junction was the scene of one of the earliest accidents on the line, in 1878, when a

southbound goods train driver mistook the junction signals and realized his mistake too late to stop his train fouling the junction. A passenger train from Morecambe hit the goods engine a glancing blow, knocking it over.

As the train climbs the tall embankment up to **Settle**, the green dome of Giggleswick school chapel can be seen to the west with Giggleswick Scar as a backdrop. The rate of climb can be judged by the increasing difference in altitude between the S&C and the Lancaster line. Settle is one of the few stations on the S&C that has generated a substantial amount of passenger and goods traffic. A market town since its charter was granted in 1249, Settle was dismissed in the eighteenth century by the Welsh traveller Thomas Pennant as resembling 'a shabby French town'. It became a staging post for coaches between York and Lancaster, and was the birthplace of George Birkbeck, who gave his name to the London university college.

The station is well sited for an easy walk into the town centre, and it is the kind of intimate town, full of narrow streets, courtyards and alleys, that is best explored on foot. The oldest building is Preston's Folly of 1675; built by Thomas Preston to impress the neighbours, it led to his bankruptcy. The peculiar arches over its doors are typical of the area.

In the Pig Yard Museum on Castle Hill can be seen the remains of animals, some extinct, that were found in Victoria Cave below the imposing cliffs of Attermire Scar to the east of the town. The museum also contains Iron Age artefacts found in the cave. A good introduction to the history and geography of the area is given by the Museum of North Craven Life in Chapel Street.

Sir Edward Elgar was a regular user of the station when he came to visit Dr Charles Buck, whose home in Market Square is now occupied by the National Westminster Bank. The stationmaster in those days was responsible for paying the wages of staff at other stations besides Settle, and these would be collected from the bank by one of the porters using a wheelbarrow to carry the wages' box. The goods yard was one of the line's busiest, and horses for the railway carts were stabled below the huge water tank that still stands at the end of the station drive.

The station building itself is one of only two structures on the S&C built to the large design, having three gabled pavilions decorated with attractive bargeboards. The footbridge was erected as recently as 1993, having been brought from Drem east of Edinburgh. The signal box still stands to the south-east of the station, but is no longer in use.

Preserved LMS Jubilee class 4-6-0 No. 45596 Bahamas enters Hellifield with a special train from Skipton to Appleby. This class of locomotive provided the swansong of express steam on the S&C under British Railways in the mid-1960s.

One of the S&C's more recent and unusual accidents occurred half a mile north of Settle station, at 01.48 on the night of 21 January 1960. Snow driven by high winds made conditions difficult but it was not heavy enough to impede traffic. The 21.05 sleeping car express from Glasgow St. Enoch to St. Pancras was being driven from Glasgow by a returning Leeds crew. The driver checked the temperature of bearings on the Britannia Pacific No. 70052 *Firth of Tay* at Dumfries and found all well. The locomotive made good progress on the climb from Carlisle to Ais Gill, recovering two late minutes with its eight-coach train. However, having topped the summit, the driver heard a regular knock which he thought was from a bearings between the wheels. He stopped the train at Garsdale and walked round the engine with a small torch, but in the blizzard he was unable to find the fault and proceeded at slow speed, after alerting the signalman to the problem. As the train neared Settle, the fireman shouted that sparks were flying from the right-hand side of the locomotive, and the driver made an emergency brake application.

The unique British Railways Pacific No. 71000 Duke of Gloucester, with Caprotti valve gear storms past Settle Junction in 1993.

Left: Class 47 No. 47721 crosses Sherrif Brow bridge to the north of Stainforth with a northbound 'Royal Scotsman' for Carlisle and Stirling in 1995.
Right: Southern Railway Pacific No. 34092 City of Wells in Stainforth cutting.

Just at that moment, a northbound goods train passed by the slowing express, and the Britannia began juddering and came to a stop. The crew on the goods felt a lurch as it passed the express, followed by the engine coming off the rails. As the crews got down from their engines, it was soon evident that they had been involved in a serious accident. The guard and fireman of the goods train ran back to Settle signal box to summon the emergency services; despite the hour, the first ambulance arrived within 17 minutes, at 02.05.

Five people were killed as a result of an extraordinary mechanical failure and unfortunate coincidences. Part of the Britannia's outside rods that transmit power from the cylinders to the wheels had gradually broken free on the climb up to Ais Gill and had been flailing round, digging into the track ballast on the opposite track. This caused the derailment of the goods train, whose locomotive fell to the right and ripped open the sides of three express carriages.

Between Settle and Stainforth the line enters the Yorkshire Dales National Park, which was set up in 1954 to give added protection to one of England's most outstandingly beautiful areas. The S&C runs through the park at the northern boundary and to the south of Kirkby Stephen.

The first commercial traffic over the S&C was lime and limestone dispatched from the Craven Lime Co.'s works at Stainforth Sidings, the remains of which can be made out on the right, under the lea of the imposing cliffs of Winskill Scar. Traffic began in 1873, the date borne in white bricks on the tall chimney that once stood near the signal box. The quarries closed in the 1950s. One September afternoon in 1961, the signalman at Stainforth had a very nasty experience, when runaway wagons demolished the bottom of his signal box.

Past the village of Stainforth the line crosses a pair of three-arch bridges, in quick succession, across a loop in the River Ribble in the infancy of its meandering course towards the sea west of Preston.

To the north of Helwith Bridge, which carries a road over both railway and river, were sidings on the west side for the Ribblesdale Lime Co's quarries on Moughton Fell, reached by an inclined plane railway. The valley opens out as the railway approaches **Horton-in-Ribblesdale** and the jelly-mould shape of Penyghent (694 m/2,276 ft) comes into view to the north-east. Just before the station on the west side were the sidings of Horton Lime Works, set up in the 1880s by a Norfolkman and which became part of ICI. The village of Horton lies to the east of the railway. Its oldest building is St. Oswald's church, which has a

Norman doorway, and the riverside Crown Hotel makes a good base for walkers – the Pennine Way passes through the village. The station is used by walkers intent on climbing the famed Three Peaks of Penyghent, Whernside (736 m/2,414 ft) and Ingleborough (724 m/2,375 ft), which calls for the stamina to ascend 1448 m (4,750 ft) and cover 24 miles. The ascent of Ingleborough is made particularly rewarding because of the remains of an Iron Age fort on its summit; sections of wall and the foundations of first-century circular huts may be seen. The area is also a Mecca for pot-holers.

The stone-built shelter on the northbound platform won the 1996 Railtrack Award for the best restored Railtrack station by a third party. The award was made to the Friends of the Settle–Carlisle Line who carried out the work with funding

LMS Class 5 4-6-0 No. 5305 passes Selside with a Carlisle-bound train in 1980. There was a petition for a station here, but only a signal box was built.

LNER A4 Pacific No. 4498 Sir Nigel Gresley passes Selside northbound in 1994.

help from the Railway Heritage Trust and the Yorkshire Dales National Park. In common with all the unstaffed stations on the S&C, a telephone is thoughtfully provided for waiting passengers to talk to a railway official to check the state of train operations – especially necessary in inclement weather, when a wait in the local hostelry may be preferable to a cold waiting-room.

As the train heads north, the landscape becomes progressively wilder, with fewer, wind-stunted trees and thinning signs of habitation, the occasional building more likely to be a small barn than a farm. The grass is still good enough for pasture, the fields still delineated by stone walls, but these too diminish as green gives way to pale brown as the dominant colour. To the west, as the train passes the hamlet of Selside, the hills form a series of sharply contoured steps leading up to South House Moor and the summit of Ingleborough. There was once a signal box at Selside, but requests for a station were turned down.

The approach to Ribblehead is marked by a row of cottages on the right-hand side that resembles railway accommodation; Salt Lake Cottages were built for workers in the similarly named quarry on the opposite side of the line.

Ribblehead–Garsdale

Ask someone to name a place on the Settle & Carlisle and the chances are it will be Ribblehead. The reason for its fame or notoriety, depending on one's viewpoint, is the eponymous viaduct that lies to the north of the station. It was well known for its dramatic, windswept location long before it became the focus of a national cause célèbre, *when British Rail used its poor condition and exaggerated estimates of repair costs as a pretext for closure of the whole railway (see pages 36–7).*

Ribblehead, or Batty Moss as it was known in the railway's early years, after the hollow spanned by the viaduct, also gained a reputation for being the site of what was probably the most grim of the navvy camps along the S&C. The shanty town was once a home of sorts to 2,000 navvies, served by a makeshift post office, school, library and, most necessary of all, hospital. The fatalities caused by accidents and smallpox obliged the Midland to contribute £20 for the enlargement of the graveyard at Chapel-le-Dale in 1871, and a plaque in the church commemorates the navvies.

A journalist from the *Lancaster Guardian* visited the camp beside the Ingleton road in 1874:

'Making our way to Batty Green one could not but look with astonishment at the numerous huts which covered the moor, and are known as Batty Green, Sebastopol, Jerusalem, Jericho, and Tunnel huts. At the first mentioned place there are Sunday and day schools, a mission house, a public library, post office, public houses, and shops for the sale of a variety of merchandise, and a new and neat looking hospital with a covered walk for convalescent patients. All is life and bustle at this moorland town of huts, potters' carts, traps and horses for hire, drapers' carts, milk carts, green grocers' carts, butchers' carts, and brewers' drays; in addition to which may be seen numerous pedestrian hawkers plying from hut to hut their different trades.'

Standing on the exposed platforms of the station today it is hard to visualize such a scene; apart from the Station Inn at the foot of the drive, there is little beside the railway to suggest that the landscape has been touched by human interference. Yet until the mid-1980s the quarry near the station was sending

out stone by rail, and the station itself was a centre of local life until it lost its staff in 1968. From 1880 until 1956 church services were held in the booking hall, and from 1938 hourly weather reports were telephoned to the Air Ministry Weather Station at Dishforth, also in Yorkshire.

One of the eight stations reopened in 1986, Ribblehead has since seen more passengers than it ever had before closure in 1970. The publicity given to the viaduct during the campaign to prevent closure, coupled with the wonderful walks to be made from the station – the Dales Way actually passes underneath the viaduct – have encouraged many to use the station. Unfortunately the northbound platform had been removed in 1974 so that a new siding for the quarry could be built; a new platform built in keeping with the Midland style was opened in May 1993.

Leaving Ribblehead station on a tall embankment, the line becomes a single track and curves gently to the right on to the viaduct. The camp beneath its 24 arches was in being for seven years while the men living there toiled on the viaduct and Blea Moor Tunnel to the north. It is little wonder that there were days when the wind was so fierce that no work could be done on the viaduct for fear of men being blown off; wind speeds of over 145 kmh (90 mph) have been recorded by the anemometer. Since opening, railwaymen crossing the viaduct in high wind have been forced to do so on their hands and knees. In steam days firemen would try to build up the fire before approaching the viaduct, because the wind could blow the coal off the shovel. Cars have been blown off trains, to be smashed on the ground below, and on one extraordinary occasion a track ganger had his cap blown off, only for it to sail under an arch

LNER A4 Pacific No. 4498 Sir Nigel Gresley crosses Ribblehead Viaduct with a northbound train. In addition to railway duties, the stationmaster at Ribblehead from 1938 had to file hourly weather reports from 07.00 until 21.00. In the first year of records, 278 cm (109½ in) of rain fell.

and land on his head again, but the wrong way round! As he concluded in narrating the incident, 'Thou can't have ivverything.'

Ribblehead Viaduct is the largest on the line, though the number of arches was not finally decided until December 1872. The foundation stone was laid on 12 October 1870 by William H. Ashwell, who was the Midland's agent on the contract and went on to become consulting engineer to the Queensland Government. It took five years to complete the viaduct which is 405 m (1,328 ft) long and 32 m (104 ft) high, with foundations going down a further 19 m (61 ft).

North of the viaduct stands one of Britain's loneliest signal boxes, Blea Moor. It is almost a mile from the nearest road, so until the age of the motor

Two diverted Class 47s meet on Ribblehead Viaduct: on the left a Euston-Glasgow train is headed by No. 47518 while the southbound equivalent is hauled by No. 47444. The track over the viaduct is now singled to reduce stresses.

car, most signalmen lived in the small row of now derelict cottages behind the box. Despite its remoteness, the signalmen were seldom lonely, since goods trains were often put into the sidings to allow faster trains to pass, their locomotives taking water while they waited for the road. Loops with facing points replaced sidings from December 1941 when a new signal box replaced the previous 1914 structure on the west side of the line. Water columns were fed from nearby tanks taking their water off Whernside, and it was a struggle during winter to prevent them freezing up. Gangers had the unenviable task of stoking the stoves beneath them. Drivers of trains that needed to take water at Blea Moor – almost invariably goods trains – would give one long and three short whistles when passing Horton northbound or Dent southbound, so that the signalman at Blea Moor could be forewarned and set the road accordingly. Crews of northbound trains that wanted a through run to the summit at Ais Gill dreaded being looped at Blea Moor, and would whistle furiously in protest if they saw the distant signal at caution. Restarting a heavy train through the

The view of Ribblehead seen by generations of footplatemen, though seldom along the boiler of an A4 Gresley Pacific, in this case No. 60023 Golden Eagle in 1963.

curves back on to the main line and against a 1 in 100 gradient called for great skill, especially in wet weather.

Blea Moor was sometimes a crew-changing point, and in bad weather special gangs would be called in, partly to check sheets on the wagons of northbound goods trains. These would often have been loosened by the wind tearing across Ribblehead Viaduct, so their ropes would need tightening. Trains of lime needed careful attention, since wet lime would smoulder and burn the wagon sides. All these railwaymen would call at the box for instructions, or to avail themselves of the stove and water supply.

It was one of the facing points installed at Blea Moor loops in 1941 that caused the derailment of the southbound Thames–Clyde Express in April 1952. The front end of a brake rod on the tender of the leading engine, a Midland Compound, had come loose north of Blea Moor Tunnel. No harm occurred until it encountered an obstacle in the form of the locking bar on the points at Blea Moor. Striking the bar caused the point blades to move sufficiently to derail the Royal Scot train engine, No. 46117 *Welsh Guardsman*,

and the leading coaches. Despite the speed at which the train was travelling, no passengers were killed.

Once past the loops at Blea Moor, the line enters a deep cutting on the approach to Blea Moor Tunnel. The climb from Settle Junction is almost over. Soon after entering the tunnel, the line levels and then begins to fall gently towards the northern portal. The 2,403 m (2,629 yd) tunnel was the most difficult single engineering feat on the line, absorbing £1.25 million of the eventual £3.3 million cost. Seven shafts were sunk, four of them equipped with winding engines; with the two tunnel entrances, this produced sixteen headings. Twelve-hour shifts were worked from 22.00 on Sunday to 22.00 on Saturday, and the rock was so hard that every inch had to be blasted. The cuttings at each end proved troublesome, too, causing the tunnel to be longer than the original survey suggested would be necessary.

Immaculately turned out LNER A3 Pacific No. 4472 Flying Scotsman emerges from the northern portal of Blea Moor Tunnel.

The dank smell of the tunnel made it unpleasant for railwaymen – and passengers who had not closed the windows. Despite the three ventilation shafts adapted from the original construction shafts, engine smoke took a long time to clear, especially on still days. Track gangs recalled that on windless days during the wars, when there was often a train in every block section, they would be able to work in the tunnel for only 1 1/2 hours in a shift, so dense was the smoke. Wet soot dropped on to the men, and the combination of sulphur, damp and a propensity for trains to slip, increased wear on the rails to the point where they had to be replaced after just four years.

A potentially disastrous accident occurred in the tunnel in 1878 when a northbound train came to a halt within sight of the northern exit. The cause was a fault with the braking system, which had 'failed safe' and brought the train to a stand. While several of the train crew were crawling underneath the carriages in the dark to release the brakes, a following express had used the enforced stop at Blea Moor to detach the pilot engine – this manoeuvre was normally carried out at Dent Head. The signalmen in the boxes at Blea Moor and Dent Head then failed to communicate with either good sense or according to strict procedures. The consequence was that the second express was signalled to proceed into the tunnel. Fortunately the guard of the halted train had been walking south laying detonators, which exploded under the wheels of the engine on the second train, alerting the driver of the danger in sufficient time for him to prevent a serious accident. No injuries were caused by the 16 kmh (10 mph) collision.

The northern portal of Blea Moor Tunnel was until recently framed by the open moorland of gorse, bracken and heather that characterizes the wild southern half of the S&C. Today it has a dark and dismal collar of commercial spruce. Shortly after leaving the tunnel, the line crosses the 10-arch Dent Head Viaduct and proceeds to skirt Great Knoutberry Hill on a ledge that follows the contours to Rise Hill Tunnel. This section of line offers wonderful views to the left over the northern flank of Whernside and down picturesque Dentdale. Dent Head signal box, another isolated post, was on the west side of the line, a little to the north of the viaduct, until its closure in 1965.

In the defile spanned by Dent Head Viaduct, marble, known as black or Dent marble, was prised out of the hillside at Nixon's quarries and sawn into blocks at High Mill, which was powered by a 30 m (60 ft) waterwheel. Little remains of the buildings clustered around the viaduct that ended their working life in 1900 when Italian marble put them out of business. The small community here may account for the original proposal to site the station for Dent near the viaduct. Besides producing marble for use by monumental

Southern Merchant Navy Pacific No. 35028 Clan Line followed by an 'Ethel' generator unit heads north from Blea Moor Tunnel. The Ethels proved extremely unpopular with photographers.

masons and for fireplaces, the quarries also supplied the stone for both Dent Head and Arten Gill viaducts. The latter, crossed before reaching Dent station, is an 11-arch structure that took over four years to build and offers a lovely view to the right up the valley of Artengill Beck. Beneath one of its arches is a track that forms a walking route between Dent and Hawes.

Dent is the highest main line station in England, at 350 m (1,150 ft). The snow fences of up-ended railway sleepers that parallel the railway indicate how bad conditions can be. To the south of the station a row of stone cabins still stands; these were built to accommodate the snow gangs that struggled to keep the line open. This entailed not so much clearing the track of snow – this had to be done largely by locomotives and heavy snowploughs – as keeping signals, signal wires, point rodding, point blades and facing point locks in operable condition. Another hazard was ice on telegraph wires: a hard freeze after rain

Class 37 No. 37178 at Blea Moor during diversion of West Coast trains, 1987.

could encase the wires in a collar of ice 10 cm (4 in) thick, the weight of which would snap the cable.

It was conditions around Dent that prevented the S&C being used as a through route for about two months during the terrible winter of early 1947. Dent station was almost buried in 4 m (12 ft) drifts, and men recall walking over the roof of the waiting-room shelter on the southbound platform. The overbridge at the north end of the station was completely buried in snow. It was near Dent that a diesel-hauled Edinburgh–St. Pancras sleeping-car express became stuck in January 1963. The passengers were transferred to the rear

three coaches, which the guard managed to uncouple. A locomotive with plough fought its way through from the north and took the three carriages back to Carlisle where they proceeded south by way of the West Coast main line.

Because of the likelihood of difficulties around Dent, it was customary to place a wagon of coal in a siding before the onset of winter, so that ploughing locomotives could be based there. The crews would use the snow cabins.

The road that crosses over the railway to the north of the station is known as the 'Coal Road'; along it came coal from pits on Mossdale Moor, carried by pack-horse or cart to homes in Dent, Garsdale and Sedburgh, or burnt in local kilns to produce agricultural lime. Over the centuries the road was also worn by millions of hooves as cattle made their way from Carlisle to such cattle fairs as

Arten Gill Viaduct is one of the most spectacularly sited on the S&C. Southern Railway 4-6-0 No. 850 Lord Nelson is seen here heading south.

Kingmoor-allocated LMS Class 5 4-6-0 No. 44669 heads a northbound freight through Dent on 26 January 1963, a few days after the line had been cleared and reopened.

During the last years of British Railways steam operation, LMS Class 5 4-6-0 No. 45295 has its water tank replenished on Garsdale watertroughs. These troughs were the highest anywhere in the world, though the distinction is tempered by the small number of countries that used them.

Malham, where up to 5,000 beasts would be sold, or to the Dales to be fattened on their lusher pastures. The railway ended these droves, and new markets were built close to goods yards, like those at Kirkby Stephen and Lazonby.

Dent Town, 4 miles down the hill to the west of the station, is a cluster of gritstone-roofed cottages flanking narrow, cobbled streets. The village church of St. Andrew was founded around 1100 and has a fine set of seventeenth-century box church pews, though they were much reduced in number by an insensitive restoration in 1889.

Besides mining coal and quarrying marble, the town's trades included butter-making and horse-breeding, but its principal industry was knitting hosiery, caps and other items – the poet Southey referred to the practitioners as 'the terrible knitters of Dent'. The industry began to fail from the mid-nineteenth century, but it is still practised in the dale and has been augmented in recent years by glass-blowing and engraving.

Dent was the birthplace of the pioneering geologist Adam Sedgwick (1785–1873), whose life is commemorated in a Shap granite fountain in the village. He became Woodwardian Professor of Geology at Cambridge and is buried in Trinity College chapel.

Leaving Dent, the station master's house can be seen to the left of the line at the entrance to the station drive; the exposed building was an early pioneer of double glazing. The cutting to the north of Dent on the approach to Rise Hill

Tunnel was notorious for drifting snow, though it is now sheltered by a depressingly uniform conifer plantation. The tunnel itself was one of the worst tasks for the railway's builders, primarily because the rock proved much less firm than expected. Four hundred navvies worked on it, living in a shanty town near Dent station. The track through the 1,109 m (1,213 yd) tunnel is level.

Leaving the north portal, passengers have views to the west over Baugh Fell and Garsdale, through which flows the Clough River. Some farms along this valley were once Norse settlements. A rare level section of track allowed the Midland to build the highest water-troughs in the world, at 335 m (1,100 ft) above sea level. Built at a cost of £4,396, the troughs were 509 m (1,670 ft) long and held 5–6,000 gallons; about 2,000 gallons could be picked up by a scoop under the locomotive tender. The problem of the high location was, of course, that they froze in winter, despite being steam-heated; on one occasion compacted snow on top of the troughs derailed two locomotives and a snowplough. Shortly after the site of the troughs, the railway reaches the only station on the S&C that was once a junction, Garsdale.

Garsdale– Kirkby Stephen

Garsdale was known for many years as Hawes Junction and then Hawes Junction & Garsdale. Until March 1959, trains could also head east along Wensleydale to the market town of Hawes, meeting end-on the North Eastern Railway-built branch from Northallerton on the East Coast main line. Passing through countryside now synonymous with the novels of James Herriot, the Wensleydale railway is the subject of a multi-million-pound proposal to rebuild it between Garsdale and the current railhead at Redmire, which is used by the Ministry of Defence to carry military traffic to Catterick Camp.

Today the only railway staff likely to be seen at **Garsdale** are the track gangers and perhaps a signalman – the box is sometimes switched out. Before the closure of the Hawes branch, and especially in the days when many trains required pilot engines, Garsdale was a scene of 24-hour activity. Implementation of the Midland's original plans for the place would have made it even busier. For reasons that are now hard to divine, the company's locomotive superintendent, Matthew Kirtley, intended to build an engine shed for 24 locomotives – the same size as that at Carlisle. Even when Samuel Johnson took over, he reduced the size by only 12 locomotives, and proposed building cottages for 20 enginemen. By 1875, more realistic councils had prevailed and a shed for a single engine was all that was eventually put up. Moreover, this was seldom if ever occupied by a Midland locomotive, since from 1881 the shed was leased by the North Eastern Railway which provided motive power for the passenger trains that ran from Hawes Junction to Northallerton.

Despite this reduction in status, the station was still a hive of activity, and 16 houses in three unequal terraces were provided for railwaymen and their families. The complete absence of any facilities in the district is reflected in the dependence on the railway for any social or religious occasions. Church services were held in the waiting room on the northbound platform, accompanied by a small harmonium, while the ladies waiting room contained the library. This was generously supplied with 150 books in around 1900 by two elderly ladies who had taken pity on this isolated community. Passengers who looked as though they could be trusted not to run off with a book were allowed to use the library while waiting for their connections. Few places in Britain can have had a more bizarre 'community hall': the space that fulfilled this function was in the stone base of the water-tank house to the south-east of the station. Here, whist drives, suppers, concerts and dances were held, to music supplied by a piano or, from the First World War, a gramophone. There was even a small stage. Until television gradually stifled such gregarious habits, these railway social events were the focus of the community and the few non-railway people in the locality were made welcome.

Despite the provision of 16 houses, the accommodation was evidently inadequate, especially when engineering work was in progress in the area: a ganger who had one of the three-bedroomed houses used to augment his income by hiring out lodgings for six men – two to a bed – while he and his wife made do with a cupboard under the stairs.

Opposite: LNER A4 Pacific No. 4498 Sir Nigel Gresley approaching Shotlock Hill Tunnel with a northbound excursion Cumbrian Mountain Express in 1994. This sister engine to the famous Mallard, holder of the world speed record for steam, has been a regular performer on excursions over the S&C .

The exposed position of Garsdale led to a classic railway story, which some have suggested may be apocryphal. During a storm at the turn of the century, an engine crew attempted to turn a locomotive on the turntable which was to the north of the station, on the west side of the line close to the point at which the Hawes branch went off. The story goes that the wind caught the engine and propelled it round like the sails of a windmill. The only way that the railwaymen could stop its rotation was to throw ballast into the pit. Certainly the wind can blow with extraordinary ferocity across the surrounding moors: in 1937 a railway magazine related an occasion when the stationmaster was quite unable to walk against the wind. Whatever the veracity of the turntable story, the perimeter of the pit was provided with a stockade of upright sleepers to provide some shelter; sceptics of the wind story say that the stockade was to help to keep the pit free of drifting snow. The turntable itself was rescued by the Keighley & Worth Valley Railway and is now in use at Keighley.

Hawes Junction has the unfortunate distinction of having been the scene of two accidents; though the second took place about a mile or so north of the junction, its genesis took place at the station. The first mishap took place in 1891, when the station was controlled by two signal boxes. Through the carelessness of the station master and the engine crew, an excursion train from Bradford to Aysgarth on the Hawes branch was accidentally backed with force into a dead end. Although all eleven carriages were damaged, only one person was seriously injured.

By the time of the next, much more serious accident, the two signal boxes had been replaced by the existing box on the northbound platform, which opened in 1910. It was in this newly opened box that the poor signalman, Alfred Sutton, realized his ghastly error and that there was nothing he could do to avert a collision – a more terrible mental anguish would be hard to imagine.

The night of 23 December 1910 was one of driving rain and strong winds, reducing visibility and making it unpleasant for engine crews trying to shelter in their cabs of minimalist design. At that time the small engine policy of the Midland meant that most passenger trains had to be assisted up to Ais Gill summit from either direction. The pilot engine would be detached and run into a siding to wait for an opportunity to run south to Hawes Junction where it would turn; often two or more pilots would couple together to make the three-mile journey. After turning at Hawes Junction, locomotives would then wait for an interval in traffic to return to their home sheds at Carlisle, Hellifield or Leeds.

In the approach to Christmas, extra trains were running to cope with the high seasonal demand, and it had been a busy shift for Sutton, who had come on duty at 20.00 on the 23rd. The succession of passenger and goods trains had been such that by 04.50 on the 24th, he had received from Ais Gill nine pilot engines; two had already turned and were in the Hawes branch platform waiting a path, while the other seven were in the sidings near the turntable and in the process of turning.

The turntable pit at Garsdale is passed by northbound Class 47 No. 47533, taken when the former junction signal box was normally switched out. The turntable has long lost its timber stockade, but the table itself survives in use at Keighley.

In clear winter light, Leeds-bound Class 156 No. 156491 passes the site of the water tower at Garsdale which was once the small settlement's community hall.

Sutton was anxious to find paths for the light engines to return home, but the offer of another southbound goods from Ais Gill and a northbound special express from Dent made it difficult to dispatch any of the waiting engines. One of the drivers added to the pressure on Sutton by wanting him to organize a relief driver, having been on duty for longer than the prescribed number of hours. Sutton then made his first error. To make room for more light engines in the Hawes platform line, he moved two Carlisle-bound 4-4-0s on to the northbound main line, instead of using empty siding space. The two engines proceeded up to the advanced starting signal and waited. Under the rule book, their engine crews should have alerted the signalman once sufficient time had elapsed for the preceding northbound express to have reached Ais Gill and so allow the signal to be cleared for them. Doubtless the weather discouraged any

of the crew from making the walk back to the signal box, and the heavy rain would probably have obscured them from the view of Sutton. None the less they could and should have given a reminding whistle.

Sutton knew yet another Class A goods train was waiting at Ais Gill, but in his desperation to clear some of the engines, he telephoned his colleague at Ais Gill to ask if he could dispatch two Leeds engines without delaying the goods. The answer was 'no', so he accepted the goods. A few minutes later he was offered by the Dent signalman the sleeping-car express from St. Pancras. Forgetting all about the two engines waiting at the advanced starter, Sutton

offered the express to Ais Gill, had it accepted and lowered his signals. Having given a short whistle, which was lost on the wind, the two light engines set off at a sedate pace for Carlisle.

Three minutes later the northbound express behind a 2-4-0 and a 4-4-0 rushed past Hawes Junction signal box at 100 kmh (60 mph). Emerging from Moorcock Tunnel on the leading engine, Driver Richard Oldcorn was horrified to see a red tail lamp ahead and made an emergency brake application. A few hundred yards north of Moorcock Tunnel, Driver George Bath on the second of the light engines happened to glance back along the line, to see the headlamps of the express emerging from the tunnel and sparks shooting out of the engines' chimneys. He threw open the regulator and shouted to his fireman to hold the whistle open. These responses were too late to avoid a collision. With brakes locked on, the express came to a halt in 137 m (150 yd) after hitting the light engines, but the impact knocked them on for a further 176 m (193 yd). Of the pilot engines, two sets of tender wheels of the leading 4-4-0 left the rails and the second derailed completely. The pilot engine of the express derailed but stayed more or less in line, but the second engine

overturned. The leading two coaches telescoped and piled up against the overturned 4-4-0.

The disaster was worsened by the outbreak of fire, when locomotive coals ignited gas escaping from the ruptured lighting systems and cylinders of the carriages. Only the last two vehicles escaped the ensuing conflagration. All eight enginemen were injured, twelve people died and nine were injured. The inquiry inevitably placed the blame on Alfred Sutton, to whom the inspecting officer paid tribute for the forthright way in which he had admitted his error. It also blamed the crews of the light engines for not obeying rules, and recommended a wide range of measures, from modifications to the signalling at Hawes Junction to the fitting of cut-off valves to gas cylinders on coaches.

Leaving Garsdale, the line curves to the left and passes over the road between Hawes and Sedbergh, just after crossing a viaduct that was called Dandry Mire before assuming the name of Moorcock. This structure was not part of the original plans, but after more than 191,131 metres^3 (250,000 yards^3) of spoil had sunk into the bog without creating more than a few feet of the intended embankment, the engineers gave up and built a 12-arch viaduct over the mire.

The historic Moorcock Inn, below the level of the railway to the right, was once the focus of an annual fair at which cattle and sheep were shown as well as a valued resting place, as lyrically described by Frederick Williams in the 1870s: '. . . travellers innumerable have been wont to dismount their mountain ponies at "The Moorcock" to refresh themselves with mountain dew, perhaps the more willingly from the thought that it has been many a mile since they had such an opportunity before, and that it will be many another before they will have one again.' The inn was also the scene on the afternoon of Boxing Day 1910 of the preliminary inquiry into the Hawes Junction disaster. Decades later it became a favoured meeting place of photographers who came to record the stirring sight of steam locomotives battling 'the Long Drag'.

From the south end of the short Moorcock Tunnel, which burrows through glacial drift, the line climbs again, at a gradient of 1 in 165 on the final stretch of the ascent to Ais Gill. Around the five-arches of Lunds Viaduct was a quarry

Above left: LNER A3 Pacific No. 4472 Flying Scotsman enters Garsdale from the north. In the era of excursions behind preserved steam locomotives, Garsdale has been a regular stop for them to take water from a specially organized supply. Right: One of the most popular and successful photographic positions on the S&C has been the vantage point to the north of Garsdale overlooking Dandry Mire Viaduct. Here LMS Pacific No. 46203 Princess Margaret Rose shows why.

from which stone for a number of structures was taken. A little further to the north is Grisedale Crossing footbridge, close to the site of the 1910 accident. The climb eases through Shotlock Hill Tunnel to reach a level stretch on the approach to the now deserted summit of Ais Gill, the highest on an English main line at 356 m (1,169 ft) above sea level. Here trains requiring assistance usually stopped to detach the pilot engine, using a pair of sidings and a crossover. During the snows of 1947 an engine derailed on the crossover and had to be re-railed by the Leeds crane, adding to the tribulations of the men trying to open the line. The sidings and signal box are no more, but the latter was saved by the Midland Railway Centre and now stands at Butterley in Derbyshire.

It was in the signal box that once stood on the west side of the line, in the small hours of a September morning in 1913, that signalman Clemmet heard the rumble of a collision followed by 'a light rising and falling like a red mist away beyond the distant signal'. He was not responsible for the worst disaster that has occurred on the S&C, but his colleague at Mallerstang signal box further north was partly to blame.

Two closely spaced southbound expresses were due to leave Carlisle that night, at 01.35 and 01.49. The first train was 13 tons over the weight limit allowed for a Class 4 4-4-0. When Driver William Nicholson was informed of his load, he asked for an assisting engine but was told that none was available;

Opposite: LMS Pacific No. 46229 Duchess of Hamilton leaves Moorcock Tunnel and crosses Lunds Viaduct with a northbound Cumbrian Mountain Express. Below: The dramatically sited summit sidings and signal box at Ais Gill.

normally he would probably not have worried about such a small excess weight, but the Carlisle shed at that time was suffering from poorly screened coal from Naworth colliery to the east of the border city. The amount of slack and small coals led to difficulties maintaining steam pressure. This could have an effect, not only on a locomotive's ability to keep time, but in severe circumstances could result in the train's brakes coming on through inadequate vacuum in the brake pipes. To keep the brakes off, steam locomotives were fitted with two ejectors, large and small, which used steam pressure to create a vacuum; the large ejector was used to create the required working vacuum quickly – when taking over or restarting a train, for example – while the small one maintained it. If boiler pressure falls, the small ejector may not have the capacity to keep the brakes off, thus requiring use of the large ejector, and so further increasing steam demands on an already low boiler pressure.

It was exactly these problems that beset Nicholson and his fireman, James Metcalf. They left Carlisle three minutes late and reached Ormside without undue difficulties, but once off the viaduct there, southbound trains encounter the first 1 in 100 gradient, which continues more or less without respite for the next 15 miles to the summit at Ais Gill. Nicholson had been helping Metcalf with the sluggish fire, but by Mallerstang (the signal box between Kirkby Stephen and Ais Gill) speed was down to 32 kmh (20 mph). The vacuum was so low that the large ejector had to be used to keep the brakes off. At about 02.57 the train ground to a halt 169 m (185 yd) north of Ais Gill distant signal, just half a mile from the summit of the climb, due to shortage of steam.

Meanwhile the 01.49 express had left Carlisle five minutes late. Driver Samuel Caudle had worked on the S&C ever since the line had opened, but the fireman, George Follows, was unfamiliar with the class of 4-4-0 working the train. However, they had a train 104 tons lighter than Nicholson and Metcalf, and made easy work of the steep gradients south of Ormside. At Kirkby Stephen Caudle left the footplate to oil the locomotive. In the days before mechanical lubrication, it was frequent practice for drivers to oil the running gear, standing on the running plate, while the train was on the move. Holding on to the handrails in a strong wind, as well as the movement of the engine, Caudle was still struggling round the oiling points as the train approached the Mallerstang distant signal. This was at caution, but Caudle later said he thought it was at clear. While Caudle was away from the footplate, Metcalf should have been vigilant in looking out for signals, but he was having difficulties with the right-hand injector, which forces water into the boiler.

With neither engineman preparing to halt the train at the Mallerstang home (stop) signal, the locomotive was still working hard as it neared Mallerstang box. Now it was the turn of the signalman, Sutherland, to compound the danger. In the hope of receiving the line clear from Ais Gill to allow him to lower his starting signal without bringing the train to a stand, Sutherland lowered his home signal as the second express approached, thinking the train was slowing. Realizing his error, he flung the home signal to danger and waved

Opposite: One of the rare sections of straight track on the wilder part of the S&C is at Mallerstang, where there was an isolated block post. In glorious summer light, LMS Princess Royal Pacific No. 46203 Princess Margaret Rose heads south.
Left: The grim aftermath of the Ais Gill disaster in 1913. This second accident within three years involving a serious fire spurred progress towards the replacement of wood by steel as the principal material for coach bodies.

a handlamp with red aspect at the locomotive, but to no avail. The train swept past the box and ignored the starting signal at danger.

The two signalmen knew that unless the first express reached Ais Gill within a minute or so, a collision was inevitable. On the first train, Nicholson had rashly told one of the two guards that it would take only a few minutes to raise steam to get under way again, so no action was taken to protect the train with detonators. Only when they heard the sound of a following train did a guard start walking back along the line showing a red light. On the second train, Caudle became aware that they had gone through Mallerstang without seeing the aspects of the two stop signals, but instead of slowing down he pressed on. Only when Follows realized that the two red lights he could see were not the Ais Gill signal lights but the rear of a train did Caudle shut the regulator and apply the brake. His engine struck the stationary train at about 48 kmh (30 mph).

Both signalmen heard the awful sound and summoned the emergency services. Seven minutes later fireman Metcalf staggered into Ais Gill signal box to confirm the tragedy. From the last three carriages of the first express, sixteen people were killed or subsequently died from their injuries. Fire broke out, more from engine coals igniting wooden carriage bodies than from escaping gas – the cut-off valves fitted in the wake of the Hawes Junction accident seemed to work.

The findings of the inquiry placed the blame largely on Caudle, who spent the rest of his railway career moving engines within the confines of Durran Hill engine shed in Carlisle. It recommended changes to the construction of carriages, discarding wood in favour of steel, the replacement of gas lamps by electric lighting, and various improvements to safety equipment carried on trains and information about their location.

As the railway begins the descent to Carlisle, it crosses over the four arches of Ais Gill Viaduct. The line is overshadowed to the west by the imposing millstone grit flank of Wild Boar Fell (708 m/2,324 ft), on which the last wild boar was reputedly killed in 1464 by Sir Richard Musgrave, whose tomb is in Kirkby Stephen parish church. The area is known as Mallerstang Common, and the signal box here was one of the remotest on the line, a steep walk up the hillside and across the River Eden from the Hawes–Kirkby Stephen road that parallels the railway. The signal box closed in 1969.

The valley of the River Eden is quite different in character from the desolate moorland to the south. The lower areas are grazed, and tree-sheltered farms and isolated barns punctuate the landscape at regular intervals. Herdwick sheep, championed by Beatrix Potter, are the dominant breed.

Overlooking the River Eden on its west bank, and clearly visible from the train, is Pendragon Castle, a twelfth-century tower with walls so thick that they contain passages. The picturesquely sited castle was once held by one of Thomas à Becket's murderers, Sir Hugh de Morville. It was burnt by the Scots in 1341 and 1541 and restored in 1660 by Lady Anne Clifford who acquired the dale in the second half of the seventeenth century. She spent the Christmas of 1663 at the castle, but the building is again ruinous. Legend has it that Uther Pendragon, father of King Arthur, was poisoned at an earlier fortification here.

In a reversal of the problem that confronted the engineers at Dandry Mire, the tall embankment to the west of the castle was originally intended to be a viaduct, but the impossibility of establishing firm foundations compelled its replacement by an embankment. However, it took over a year of tipping before the formation advanced a single yard. A rock cutting heralds the approach to the 388 m (424 yd) Birkett Tunnel, which is driven through the Great Pennine Fault. Within the space of a hundred metres, the tunnellers encountered shale, mountain limestone, magnesian limestone, grit, slate, iron, coal and lead ore, which Crossley described as 'the most curious combination I ever saw'.

Above the tunnel is a minor road that links the A683 with Sandpot, near Pendragon Castle; it is known locally as the 'Tommy Road' after the notorious Tommy shops where navvies on some contracts were compelled to purchase their supplies – at a good profit to the contractor. Where the road crosses the tunnel, remains can be seen of the camp used by navvies working on the tunnel. Leaving the tunnel a new panorama to the north and west opens up across the broad, gently undulating and fertile valley towards Brough and Stainmore Common.

A mile or so to the south of Kirkby Stephen, though not visible from the railway, lies Wharton Hall, built in stages from the fifteenth century round a courtyard. Mary Queen of Scots was entertained here in 1568 by the Second Baron Wharton while she was on her way to Castle Bolton, and in 1617 James I was given so lavish a reception by Philip, Third Baron Wharton that the latter was reduced to straightened circumstances. Philip's great grandson, Thomas, First Marquis of Wharton (1648-1715), was less flattering to James I's grandson: he composed the famous song 'Lilliburlero' in 1687, later boasting that it had 'sung James II out of three kingdoms'. Thomas went on to become lord-lieutenant of Ireland between 1708 and 1710, and a portrait of him by Sir Godfrey Kneller hangs in the National Portrait Gallery.

Class 47 No. 47049 heads a southbound freight over the four-arch Ais Gill Viaduct with a train of oil and cement wagons. Freight traffic over the line is now reviving.

A remarkable portrait of Thomas's father – Philip, Fourth Baron Wharton – has achieved international prominence. During the 1630s, Philip was a prominent member of court and became one of Van Dyck's principal patrons, constructing a gallery in his house at Upper Winchendon near Aylesbury to display his collection of twelve portraits by Van Dyck; the number grew to 32. The collection was sold in 1725 by Philip's grandson, the First Duke of Wharton, to the Prime Minister, Sir Robert Walpole, who hung them at Houghton Hall in Norfolk. In a highly criticized move, George Walpole sold most of them in 1779 to Catherine the Great of Russia. The Wharton portrait was one of a number of paintings sold by the Soviet Union in the 1920s to the USA, and it now hangs in the National Gallery of Art in Washington.

Near Wharton Hall is an exceptionally good example of strip lynchets, hillside terraces that were made during medieval times when pressure for more cultivated land grew. Wharton can be reached by a footpath from main road that links Kirkby Stephen station with the town.

Opposite: LNER A4 Pacific No. 4468 Mallard passes Birkett Common with a southbound excursion. The Mallard is one of the more famous locomotives to travel on the S&C because it holds the land speed record for a steam locomotive, which it took in 1938 by travelling 201 kmh (126 mph).
Below: LNER A4 Pacific No. 60009 Union of South Africa leaves Birkett Tunnel at speed.

Kirkby Stephen–Appleby

*The station at **Kirkby Stephen** is situated on a hill a mile above the linear market town built on the west bank of the River Eden. On the route of Wainwright's Coast-to-Coast walk, Kirkby Stephen was once served by an east–west railway running from Darlington to Tebay and to Penrith, which had been opened in the 1860s and closed in 1962. Part of the North Eastern Railway (NER), the railway was notable for its dramatically sited viaducts of tapering ironwork – there has even been a suggestion that lottery money might be used to reconstruct one.*

The NER station was closer to the town centre and retained a good share of the district's agricultural traffic, to the Midland's chagrin. The size of the goods shed and three-gabled station is indicative of the company's largely unfulfilled expectations.

Kirkby Stephen market is held on Monday in a square that was once host to the dubious pastime of bull-baiting; the area is marked by a ring of cobblestones, but the practice was stopped after 1820 when a bull broke free. Probably the busiest day of the year is the October Luke Fair, a cattle and sheep sale that generated heavy traffic for the railway. Local boys would hire themselves out on droving duties for the day, raising money to buy fireworks. In moving animals between the market and the two stations, inquisitive cows were known to enter houses whose owners had thoughtlessly left the front door open, with odiferous results.

The cloisters between the market square and the church were put up for shelter as a philanthropic gesture by a navy purser named John Waller who was born in the town. The oldest parts of the much-rebuilt church, which is shared by Anglicans and Catholics, date from the early thirteenth century. The nave of the parish church dates from 1220, the tower from around 1500. Unusually the church is not dedicated to any saint, and its great treasure is an eighth-century representation of Loki, the Norse god of strife and spirit of evil; in accordance with legend, he is depicted in chains. It is the only such stone in England, and only one other is known to survive in Europe. The church includes the family chapels of the Whartons and Musgraves.

Leaving Kirkby Stephen the rows of houses built by the Midland for its employees can be seen on each side of the line beside the A685 road which the line crosses. Curving round to the west, the line crosses Scandal Beck by the 12-arch Smardale Viaduct, which has the distinction of being the highest on the Midland, at 39 m (130 ft). The foundations for the 60,000 tons of grey limestone and millstone grit used in the viaduct had to be sunk 14 m (45 ft) below the river. When the viaduct was finished after $4^1/_2$ years' work, the contractors asked the wife of John Crossley to lay the last stone; it bears the inscription 'This last stone was laid by Agnes Crossley, June 8th, 1875.' Midland passengers would often have seen a goods train on the Kirkby Stephen to Tebay line that once passed beneath the viaduct; the route carried prodigious quantities of coke from County Durham to the blast furnaces of west Cumberland, while finished products such as pig iron, rails and girders travelled the other way.

The short Crosby Garrett Tunnel is soon followed by the six-arch viaduct that dominates the village. For some reason the station here had a particularly

In conditions that attract scores of photographers, Midland Compound No. 1000 and LMS Jubilee 4-6-0 No. 5690 Leander head south over Smardale Viaduct in 1983. The 12-span structure is the second longest on the line after Ribblehead and once crossed over the North Eastern Railway's line from Darlington to Tebay.

A northbound train behind Class 45 No. 45143 crosses Smardale Viaduct. The viaduct crosses Scandal Beck which joins the River Eden to the east of Soulby.

long platform; it was more likely to assist in the loading of milk, since the · station closed to passengers as early as 1952 through lack of patronage. A signalman at Crosby Garrett was largely responsible for a mishap to an excursion train returning from Edinburgh to Rochdale on a July night in 1888. Although the train was booked to be shunted into a siding at either Kirkby Stephen or Mallerstang to allow a Scotch express to overtake it, a decision was taken to shunt the excursion out of the way at Crosby Garrett, at 01.04. The 19-coach excursion was considerably longer than a normal passenger train, but the two guards did not inform the signalman of the fact, and the signalman never thought to ask. Although the train was too long for the siding, the accident would not have happened were it not for muddled signals and actions by the two guards and a railway inspector from Rochdale. The upshot was that the train rammed the buffer stops, injuring seven passengers and the inspector.

The station at Crosby Garrett was one of the few on the S&C that was perfectly sited for accessibility. The few houses cluster round the piers of the

Class 47 No. 47077 crosses Crosby Garrett Viaduct with a northbound train. The station closed in 1952, despite being well sited for the small community.

viaduct, from which can be seen, built on a steep hill for defensive reasons, the Church of St. Andrew. It is thought to be Anglo-Saxon in origin though the greater part of the building dates from an enlargement around 1175, and the projecting bell-turret on the west front was probably added in the thirteenth century. Cairns are to found on several of the surrounding hills.

The countryside is now much more open, with views to the west as far as the Lake District peaks. The rich pasture speaks of the milk traffic that was once a good source of revenue for the railway. Two miles north of Crosby Garrett the line crosses Griseburn Viaduct of seven arches. The viaduct piers are built of stone, but the arches were formed of bricks made on the site. A little further to the north is the site of Griseburn Ballast Sidings, where the signal box closed in 1981. The sidings were the scene of an unusual incident one November night in 1948, when work had finished re-railing some wagons

using a 50-ton breakdown crane. The crane was standing on the northbound line, on the 1 in 100 gradient, when it was nudged by the locomotive to which it was about to be coupled. The crane brakes had not been properly applied, and the crane began to descend the gradient. Sadly a railwayman was killed in the futile attempt to stop the heavy crane, which ran on, 'right line', as far as Lazonby, 23 miles away.

From Griseburn the Helm Beck is in view to the right, forming a very attractive stretch of line down to Helm Tunnel, the name being given to the

Right: With a train of typical length for the time, Class 45/1 No. 45108 crosses Crosby Garrett Viaduct with the 16.37 Leeds–Carlisle train on 29 June 1983. Below: Class 47 No. 47475 heads a train for Leeds through the site of Crosby Garrett station in 1990. Considerable quantities of milk were once loaded here.

Class 47 No. 47634 Henry Ford leaves the south portal of Helm Tunnel between Crosby Garrett and Ormside. A grocer from Carlisle opened a store to supply the navvies living in a camp near the tunnel, where the contractor provided a reading-room, coffee-house and hospital.

Opposite: LMS Jubilee 4-6-0 No. 45596 Bahamas heads a Carlisle-Oxenhope special near Ormside in 1992. The last Jubilees to operate expresses over the S&C under British Ralways were well recorded, often by photographers who had spent hours cleaning the locomotives prior to leaving the locomotive depot.

wind which can blow with particular ferocity hereabouts. Crossing an embankment, the line passes the site of Ormside station, which is just over half way between Settle and Carlisle. The station closed in 1952, the signal box eight years later. It was here, in the small hours of an August night in 1876, that the very first accident on the S&C occurred. The Ormside signalman received warning from Crosby Garrett that a northbound goods train had split in two. At the same moment he was offered by the Appleby signalman a Carlisle to St. Pancras express. The Ormside signalman should have stopped the express and allowed the goods a clear run, warning the driver by a handlamp signal that his train was divided. Instead he decided to stop both trains, but when the express arrived first he made a second error in allowing it to proceed with caution. At that point the first part of the goods passed the locomotive of the express, but a moment later the second section caught up the leading wagons and collided. Some of the wagons derailed, catching the side of the passing carriages and injuring two passengers and a guard.

The village of Ormside is just to the east of the line. At the far end of the village close to the river and hall is the Church of St. James, which has an eleventh-century doorway and a tower obviously built for defence. Almost 200 years ago the richest known example of Anglo-Saxon metalwork was found in the churchyard; made in the ninth century, it is called the Ormside Bowl and can be seen in York Museum.

A little to the north the line crosses the now broad River Eden by the ten-arched Ormside Viaduct, the start of a rare section of rising gradient towards Appleby. There is a view west from the viaduct over a bend in the Eden, which flows north-west through Carlisle to join the Solway. Over to the right the remnants of the Darlington–Kirkby Stephen–Penrith line come into view as it swings in from Warcop and the army camp that the truncated branch served long after the rest of the line closed in 1962. The final approach to Appleby is marked on the east side of the line by a large dairy which opened in 1931 as the Express Dairy and was rail-connected. At first the glass-lined milk tanks bound for London were attached to an afternoon train, but as traffic built up, it became a special working with up to 27 tanks a day being dispatched. During the 1950s the factory turned over to cheese production.

Appleby–Carlisle

Once the county town of Westmorland, Appleby is built around a large loop in the River Eden and was granted a charter by Henry I on the same day as the privilege was bestowed on York. Its historic importance is reflected in a former population of 11,000; today it has 2,400. At its centre is a long rectangular market place known as Boroughgate, which is marked at its upper end by High Cross and by the castle which is clearly visible from the station above the rooftops.

Dominating the town, Appleby Castle was in being by 1120 but it is impossible to date precisely the start of work. In 1174 it fell to the invading Scots army of William the Lion. The oldest part is the twelfth-century, square-plan stone keep, topped by four turrets, though the sandstone curtain walls also date from that century. The Clifford family became its owners in the late thirteenth century, and Lady Anne Clifford restored the keep, which is larger than William I's White Tower at the Tower of London. The east range was rebuilt in 1686–8 by Lady Anne's son-in-law, the Earl of Thanet, using stone from Brough and Brougham castles.

Today the castle is open to visitors: besides the Norman keep and Great Hall with Clifford family portraits and the painting Lady Anne commissioned to commemorate her inheritance, it has become a home for rare farm animals, under the auspices of the Rare Breeds Survival Trust, and for a large collection of wildfowl, pheasants, poultry and owls. Collections of rare bicycles and Roman armour can also be seen. A little to the north of the castle, Lady Anne built St. Anne's Hospital, a tranquil though rather austere red sandstone row of almshouses built around a courtyard in 1651–3 in the upper part of the town; it still houses retired ladies. The exceptionally broad main street has a number of fine buildings, notably the Moot Hall of 1596, where the town council has met for centuries, and the White House of 1756 on which every window has an ogee head. Little has survived the destructive raids of the Scots – the town was almost completely burned down in 1388 – but the street plan remains medieval even if the town has a Georgian and Victorian appearance.

At the lower end of Boroughgate is Low Cross and the Church of St. Lawrence. The bottom of the church's tower dates from Norman times, but the nave is largely around 1300 with a fifteenth-century screen. Lady Anne Clifford's family chapel was built in 1654–5; she lies here alongside her mother in a vault beneath her tomb. The organ was brought from Carlisle Cathedral in 1684, replacing one destroyed during the Civil War. The church bells were rung on the day in 1866 when news arrived of the successful passage of the S&C Bill through the House of Commons.

To the north-west of the town is the grammar school where George Washington's brothers were pupils. Market day is Saturday, but the most famous market is held only once a year, in June, when people from all over the country come to trade at the Horse Fair or to compete in trotting races.

There is an attractive riverside walk south from Appleby on a footpath beside the west bank, passing under the railway at Ormside and crossing the river by a footbridge near Ormside church. The return takes a path on the east side of the railway before crossing it by a small bridge before the town is reached.

Appleby has always been one of the most important sources of traffic on the S&C, and between 1880 and 1903 even had a local service to Penrith, timed to connect with expresses from St. Pancras and operated by the North Eastern Railway over the spur to the Eden Valley line. Appleby has long been a major cattle centre, with weekly stock auctions, and was third (to Settle and Lazonby) in the amount of livestock traffic handled by S&C stations. Prize cattle were sometimes accorded the superior comfort of horseboxes in which to travel. The goods shed is now occupied by Appleby Heritage Centre.

With the three gables given to larger stations, Appleby is unusual in being built of brick. The main buildings are on the west side, convenient for the

In 1993 an enterprising service of special trains was laid on between Carlisle and Kirkby Stephen using BR Standard Class 4MT 2-6-4T No. 80080, which is seen here on Armathwaite curve. The combination of some of Britain's finest landscapes and steam traction has made the S&C the foremost route for such excursions.

town. A plaque on the station commemorates a sad day in May 1978 when the well-known railway photographer, the Rt. Rev. Eric Treacy, formerly Lord Bishop of Wakefield, collapsed and died while waiting to photograph a steam train. A memorial service was held in September at Appleby station, at which the plaque was unveiled.

The two platforms are connected by an ornate footbridge. Until 1973 there were two signal boxes; the current box, built in 1951 to replace a burnt-out predecessor, is to the north of the station. The water tower at the south end is a reconstruction for use by steam specials, brought into use in 1991 and partly paid for through fundraising by the local Round Table.

As the train leaves Appleby and heads for Long Marton, the peculiar shapes of Dufton and Knock pikes can be seen to the east. The line crosses the Trout Beck by a five-arch bridge just before the site of Long Marton station which closed in 1970. At one time an aerial ropeway brought to the goods yard buckets of barytes from a mine on the fells to the east, depositing the loads in a hopper for onward movement by rail.

To the west of the line lies Kirkby Thore where there was a Roman fort and marching camp named Bravoniacum. No station was built to serve Kirkby Thore, but the British Gypsum works to the north-west of the village generates traffic for the railway. The principal flow is trainloads of desulphogypsum from the power station at Drax in North Yorkshire, which produces this by-product as part of the desulphurization process. A ten-year contract for this rail movement was signed in 1993.

New Biggin station closed in 1970, and the station is now a house. Frederick Williams relates a story told him by an engineer on the S&C regarding the survey and acquisition of land in the district. During a preliminary survey, he encountered the local landowner, Mr Crackmanthorpe, who inquired what they were doing. On hearing the purpose of their work, and that the intention was to drive the railway through an oak wood that belonged to him, the landowner was indignant. Realizing the likely difficulty the gentleman might pose, the engineer wisely suggested a visit from the Midland's General Manager might be in order. James Allport and John Crossley called on Mr Crackmanthorpe and clearly won him over with the benefits the railway

Opposite: Pacific No. 46229 Duchess of Hamilton crosses Long Marton Viaduct.
Below: Class 47 No. 47119 enters Appleby with a diverted train for Weston, 1982.

would confer on the area. The next meeting between the junior engineer and the landowner was marked by greater cordiality, the latter stating that he had only one condition to make. 'It is that you spare me the largest and finest oak in my wood.' The engineer readily agreed. 'Do you know what I want it for?' continued the proprietor. 'No sir, but whatever you want it for, it shall be saved,' replied the engineer. 'Well,' said Mr Crackmanthorpe good naturedly, 'it's to hang you and all the engineers of the Midland Railway upon it, for daring to come here at all!'

A four-arched viaduct takes the railway across Crowdundle Beck, which used to mark the county boundary between Westmorland and Cumberland and flows on past the National Trust garden of Acorn Bank. This seventeenth-century, 1½-acre walled garden is noted for its display of daffodils and for its herb garden, which has the largest collection of culinary and medicinal plants in the north. The manor house itself is a Sue Ryder home and is open by arrangement.

The first level crossing on the S&C is encountered at Culgaith, another station closed in 1970, but the 1908 signal box stands at the south end of the former platforms. The station was the only one on the S&C with non-standard buildings, probably because it was not opened until 1880, four years after most of the others. The station survives as a residence and has a more domestic appearance than the standard stations, which are unmistakably railway buildings even if attractively designed. The station master here had to make do with a cottage just behind the platform instead of a substantial two-storey house. There was never a goods shed here, but a significant amount of milk was sent out by rail.

There was an accident a little to the north of the station in 1930, when a ballast train and a stopping train from Hellifield to Carlisle met head-on, due to a combination of unfortunate errors by three railwaymen. The driver of the passenger train was killed, and a passenger later died in hospital. The damage done to the passenger locomotive, Claughton 4-6-0 No. 5971 *Croxteth*, was severe enough to warrant a rebuild, and the result was the first of the Patriot class.

The tunnels of Culgaith (604 m/661 yd) through hard red marl and Waste Bank (149 m/164 yd) follow in quick succession before a section that offers delightful views to the west over the meandering Eden and its confluence with the River Eamont which flows from Ullswater to the south-west of Penrith. It was to take advantage of the S&C's proximity to Ullswater and Penrith that the Midland had the road improved between **Langwathby**, the next station, and Penrith. For some years horse-drawn charabancs operated from Langwathby station during the summer months, offering tours to Ullswater. The station was

Opposite: Southbound LNER A2 Pacific No. 60532 Blue Peter at New Biggin.
Below: LNER A3 Pacific No. 4472 Flying Scotsman leaves Culgaith Tunnel on 27 July 1983. The A3 is running with the tender from A4 No. 4498 Sir Nigel Gresley.

reopened in 1986, but the beautifully kept station is now occupied by the 'Brief Encounter' café/restaurant. At first following the older spelling of the village, Langwathby station was known as Longwathby for five months after it opened in May 1876.

Only 1¹/₂ miles north of Langwathby is the closed station of Little Salkeld, preceded by a seven-arch viaduct over Briggle Beck. At the south end of the station site, the railway crosses over the minor road that has been incorporated into Sustrans's Sea to Sea cycle route from Whitehaven/Workington–Sunderland/Newcastle. Near the bridge is Little Salkeld Watermill, an eighteenth-century cornmill powered by a pair of cast-iron overshot wheels. Milling stoneground organic flours, it is open to visitors.

For such a small station, Little Salkeld seems to have been rather prone to accidents, having been the scene of no less than three. Even more oddly, two of them involved the same locomotive. The first occurred in January 1918 when a northbound express hauled by Compound 4-4-0 No. 1010 ran into a huge landslide in Long Meg cutting, only minutes after a platelayer had walked through without anything being amiss. The slip had been brought on by a thaw. Seven passengers were killed.

The next accident, in July 1933, could certainly have been avoided, and was caused by a complete disregard for regulations on the part of a porter-signalman made grumpy by having his lunch interrupted. Little Salkeld was one of the few signal boxes on the S&C that was usually switched out; that is,

Opposite: LMS Princess Royal Pacific No. 46203 Princess Margaret Rose passes Keld, just north of Appleby, with a southbound Cumbrian Mountain Express in 1994.
Below: In British Railways days, trains for Long Meg sidings generated a healthy freight traffic. LMS 8F 2-8-0 No. 48090 is seen here passing Kirkby Stephen.

the signal boxes on either side were put in direct contact and the signals at Little Salkeld were pulled off for up and down lines. The box was opened only when a goods train had to pick up or drop off wagons.

Being a quiet station, Little Salkeld no longer had a station master, and the person in charge was porter-signalman Hannah. His supervisor, the station master at Langwathby, was unaware that Hannah was in the habit of taking his lunch at 12.30, an hour earlier than he should have done, in order to oblige his landlady who regarded a 13.30 lunch as unacceptable to her regime. While having his lunch, Hannah heard the whistle of a goods train he wasn't expecting. The driver informed Hannah that he had a wagon of coal to drop off. Having had to abandon his lunch, Hannah truculently stomped off to the signal box to superintend the various shunting movements. Inexplicably he did not check with the signalmen on either side what trains were in the vicinity, nor did he inform them that he was opening the box to allow the wagon to be shunted. By moving the points, the home signals were automatically placed at danger, but not the distant signals. As the goods engine was propelling three wagons over a crossover between up and down lines, a southbound express hauled by No. 1010 came tearing out of the cutting to the north; the distant signal had shown a clear road through the station and the driver was making speed for the climb to his first stop at Appleby. The Compound struck the goods engine tender and leading wagon and derailed to the left, while the carriages careered to the right and collided with the rest of the goods train. Despite extensive damage to the carriages, no passengers were killed – carriage design and construction had improved significantly since pre-war days. However, the poor driver of the goods train, who was on the point of retirement, was fatally injured.

The final mishap at Little Salkeld was in 1961, when a northbound goods was derailed just north of the station and came into collision with a southbound goods, blocking both lines.

A little to the north-east of the village is Long Meg and Her Daughters, the second largest stone 'circle' in England – it is actually oval in plan, measuring about 110 × 93 m/360 × 305 ft. Neolithic in origin, it is thought to have once had about 70 stones, but today 27 still stand to a height of up to 2.7 m (9 ft). These are the daughters; Meg is a square stone standing 3.65 m (12 ft) high about 18.3 m (60 ft) outside the circle.

Further picturesque views are to be had of the Eden just past Little Salkeld as the line passes through parkland. Considerable traffic was once generated for the railway by Long Meg gypsum mine and plaster works to the north of Little Salkeld; the gypsum was quarried from 1875 to 1895 when it became

Preserved LMS 8F 2-8-0 No. 48151 passes Lazonby & Kirkoswald with a southbound excursion for Leeds in 1988. The once busy goods shed and yard has been taken over by a thriving bakery.

necessary to mine it. After grinding, the material was dried in coal-fired pans to produce commercial plaster of Paris. The remains of the extensive sidings that served the works can still be seen to the right, just before the line curves to the left to cross the River Eden for the last time, by means of a sandstone seven-arch viaduct. This had to be built using a cofferdam to protect the foundations, so difficult was it to find a secure footing for the piers. The river marks the transition from limestone to sandstone.

The parkland surrounding the house of Eden Lacy to the east of the line forms a beautiful setting and prompted construction of an ornamental bridge for the then landowner, Colonel Sanderson. On the right just before Lazonby Tunnel (90 m/99 yd) were Lazonby ballast sidings, where the signal box was taken out of use as long ago as 1878–9.

The now reopened station at **Lazonby & Kirkoswald** is conveniently situated for the former village, but Kirkoswald is about a mile to the east across the river. The elegant brick bridge that carries the road over the water can be seen from the railway. Kirkoswald is a good example of the impact the coming of the railway could have on commercial activity in a country district: it has a fine market square at its centre, but the long-established livestock markets once held here were moved to the station with the opening of the S&C. It became one of the busiest goods stations on the line, dominated by livestock traffic which even eclipsed that at Appleby and Settle during the period from 1916 to 1922. Trainloads of sheep from northern Scotland were received, and on stock sale days as many as 55 wagons might be sent off. Such sales naturally brought many buyers in by train, and the importance of locally based dealers was reflected in the special stopping of the northbound Scotch express at 04.30 to allow dealers to reach St. Boswells for the stock sales in the Borders town.

There were other commodities, too: three coal merchants had premises in the yard, crates of rabbits were sent to the West Riding, and timber and potatoes dispatched – vanloads of potato sacks would be received. Salmon caught in the Eden were sent to London in special boxes – anglers were allowed to keep one fish, but any more had to be sold on. Many of the fishermen were well-to-do men from Leeds and Bradford who would be met off the train at Lazonby by local ghillies.

Both villages have fine though very different churches: the Church of St. Nicholas at Lazonby was built in 1863 to the design of Anthony Salvin; the

church of St. Oswald in Kirkoswald was begun in Norman times, built at the foot of the hill to mark the site of the saint's baptisms. The son of a king of Northumbria, Oswald defeated and killed in battle near Hexham the tyrannical British king, Cadwalla, and became king of Northumbria. Oswald himself was later killed in battle in 642. A spring rises under the nave, feeding the well by the west wall of the church. The church has a separate square tower put up in the nineteenth century.

The buildings of a religious college founded in 1523 to the north of St. Oswald were put up around a fourteenth-century pele tower by Thomas de Dacre and his wife Isabel de Greystoke. After its Dissolution in 1547, it was adapted to become a house and it has been the home of the Fetherstonhaugh family for about four centuries. Little survives of a moated castle built in the

early thirteenth century except a tower. It was burnt down by the Scots in 1314, but rebuilt. Its last occupant was Lord William Howard who sold much of the materials after he moved out in 1604.

The section between Lazonby and Cotehill is particularly attractive, and has been described by some writers as the prettiest part of the Eden Valley. For several miles the river runs through a densely wooded gorge to right, precipitous slopes of birch and bracken dropping down to the water far below. The best way to enjoy this outstanding stretch of river is to walk beside it

Opposite: LNER A4 Pacific No. 4498 Sir Nigel Gresley heads north past Baron Wood, one of the most scenic parts of the line, especially in autumn.
Below: Southbound LMS Pacific No. 46229 Duchess of Hamilton at Baron Wood.

Opposite: LMS Pacific No. 6201 Princess Elizabeth threads Baron Wood in 1987. Below right: LMS Jubilee class 4-6-0 No. 45697 Achilles heads a train of Mk I stock past Cumwhinton with a Scottish tours charter train in 1965.

between Lazonby and Armathwaite, the next station north. A leaflet devoted to the Eden Gorge is available from TICs. Not to be missed on the east bank are the ancient Nunnery Walks, created near the confluence of the Eden and Groglin rivers to help walkers admire the nearby waterfalls and 61 m- (200 ft-) high sandstone cliffs. At a bend where river and railway are in close proximity is a place on the east bank known as Samson's Cave. This was named after a railway navvy who was involved in a brawl that ended in his opponent's death. Samson hid in the cave but was found, taken to Carlisle and hanged.

As well as sandstone cuttings, two tunnels interrupt the view – Baron Wood No. 1 (189 m/207 yd) and No. 2 (229 m/251 yd) – but there are more panoramas along the river as the valley broadens out and over extensive coniferous plantations before Armathwaite Tunnel, the line's last, 1½ miles south of the station. Before reaching **Armathwaite**, the line crosses a curving nine-arch viaduct. Besides the station buildings, the goods shed and signal box stand, the latter having been closed as recently as 1983 and now externally restored by Friends of the Settle–Carlisle Line. The village is just to the east of the line, though invisible from it because it is set beside the river, well below the railway. The castle, a four-storey pele tower in a glorious position by the River Eden, was adapted into a country house after it was acquired by William Sanderson in 1712, the front being a typically northern style of Early Georgian.

The Chapel of Christ and Mary has stained glass in the east window designed by Morris & Co. in 1914, though long after the deaths of William Morris and Sir Edward Burne-Jones, who had designed many of the windows produced by the company. Also in the village is the Eden Valley Woollen Mill, which is open to visitors and produces a variety of woven fabrics that can be bought by the metre or made into garments.

During construction of the railway, the people of Armathwaite witnessed one of the relatively few incidents of public disorder caused by the navvies: an Irishman was killed in a fight, and there ensued a stand-off between a hundred English navvies and the armed constabulary.

Leaving Armathwaite, the railway again looks down on the Eden, from what is, surprisingly, one of the largest embankments on the railway, made up of 305,810 m³ (400,000 yd³) of material. The river snakes its way through the pastoral landscape between tree-lined banks, but the Gorge was the climax of the S&C's scenic delights, and the views from here onwards are pleasant, but lack the scale and drama of what has gone before. The line crosses the seven-arch Dry Beck Viaduct before curving to the left to pass close to a now wooded place on the river called Eden Brows. The embankment here gave the builders great trouble, since tipping to form it merely caused the ground to slip into the river. Crossley ignored the sceptics who said that the terrain made construction of a railway an impossibility and succeeded in building the line across the slope; he did this by sinking vertical shafts that were filled with stone and thereby acted as both drains and supports to act against further slips. The embankment leads on to High Stand Gill Viaduct, which has four arches and crosses the wooded ravine that takes the stream down to the Eden.

The railway is taken over a minor road by one of the S&C's few level crossings, controlled by the oldest signal box on the line. Low House Crossing was opened in 1900, only a short distance south of Cotehill station. Closed in 1952, this station was for a short time called both High Stand Gill and

Knothill, the latter being the name of gypsum quarries and a plaster and cement works that were served by a short branch from a point directly opposite Cotehill signal box, which was also closed in 1952. Little remains to mark the site of the station apart from a row of Midland cottages. The church of 1868 at Cotehill has a most curious north-east tower with a top shaped like a stupa.

The line veers away from the Eden and passes a group of derelict sidings, but still with operating signal box. Howe & Co's Siding (actually there were numerous sidings here) dates back to the opening of the S&C, although the present box replaced the original one in 1916. A branch went off to the south-west to serve a tile works, a plaster works and several brickworks. Howe & Co.'s Siding is the 'fringe' box to Carlisle Power Signal Box and marks the end of mechanical signalling, replaced by electric colour light signals into Carlisle.

Below: Carlisle station, before the railway companies were amalgamated in 1922, was one of the most interesting places to watch trains, with the colourful liveries of eight different railways to be seen. The Midland was the latecomer, but S&C traffic compelled enlargement; although the MR was denied a place on the LNWR and CR Joint Committee which ran the station.

NBR J36 0-6-0 No. 673 Maude passes London Road Junction, Carlisle, on 17 May 1980, en route to the 150th anniversary celebrations of the Liverpool & Manchester.

A mile or so further north are the remains of Cumwhinton station, which was closed in 1956. It was near the station that a wolf was run over by an express in December 1904; the animal had escaped from private grounds in Allendale to the east of Alston and had killed about 40 sheep during its days of freedom.

Less remains of Scotby station, which was the first station on the S&C to be closed, in 1942, and the signal box was also an early economy, closing in 1909. As late as 1600 Scotby was the victim of one of the cross-border raids that had been going on for centuries; under the joint command of the Border reiver Kinmont Willie, a 140-strong band of outlaws known as Sandy's Bairns burnt and pillaged, taking prisoners and a hundred head of cattle. Now almost a suburb of Carlisle, Scotby has a church of 1854 built by Anthony Salvin.

The line from Newcastle appears to the north, and the two meet at Petteril Bridge Junction. Before the junction, the land on either side of the line was once occupied by extensive goods and carriage sidings and (on the left) by Durran Hill engine shed. This could accommodate 24 engines around a 17 m (55 ft) turntable. The shed was closed in 1936 but reopened during the Second World War and finally closed as late as 1959. The goods yard and attractive goods shed to the north of the railway after Petteril Bridge belonged to the North Eastern Railway, which owned the railway from Newcastle.

The final approach to **Carlisle** Citadel station entails a sharp curve to the right to join the West Coast main line at the south end of the station. Its imposing façade incorporating a clock-tower was designed by Sir William Tite in the late 1840s, long before the Midland arrived, using a Tudor-Gothic style to harmonize with the crenellated Citadel law courts to the left outside the station. These were designed by Sir Robert Smirke and completed in 1810–11.

Following the opening of the S&C, it was quickly apparent that Carlisle station could not cope with the trains of seven companies travelling over eight routes into the border town. Accordingly it was enlarged in 1878–81 to create new platforms and offices, covered by a ridge-and-furrow roof of almost 6 acres. The city had become one of Britain's foremost railway junctions, with more railway companies entering the city than any other city apart from the capital. Although all seven companies ran their passenger trains into Carlisle Citadel station, all had separate goods stations and most had their own engine sheds, some very large establishments. In addition, Cowan, Sheldon & Co.

Opposite: LNER A4 Pacific No. 4498 Sir Nigel Gresley at Carlisle Citadel station.

set up an engineering works in the city in 1847, becoming one of the foremost producers of railway cranes, many of which were exported all over the world.

Carlisle was founded by the Celts, and developed as Luguvalium by the Romans as a defensive base for Hadrian's Wall. There appear to have been two separate forts, and the town grew to cover about 28 ha (70 acres). Carlisle was captured from the Scots by William Rufus in 1092, when work on the castle was begun, creating a wooden palisaded enclosure on a bluff overlooking the Eden. Work began on the great tower in 1122 and was continued after the town surrendered to David I of Scotland in 1136; it was completed by 1174, when the town was besieged by William the Lion. The principal building of the castle, the tower has been greatly altered over the years – for example, it was modified during Henry VIII's reign to accept the use of heavy guns. Mary Queen of Scots was imprisoned there in 1568.

In 1292 fire destroyed most of the buildings in the city. Over four centuries later, the rebuilt city withstood a siege of nine months during the Civil War, eventually it was taken by a Scottish army in 1645. A century later Bonnie Prince Charlie proclaimed his father king at the market cross at one end of English Street, but within weeks the city had fallen to the bloody Duke of Cumberland.

The castle, open throughout the year, also played a major role in the long history of cross-border raiding and feuding, some of the culprits being interned in its dungeons. The 300-year-history of the county's regiment, the King's Own Royal Borderers, is housed in the castle, the regiment's home since 1873.

In the centre of the city is the timber-framed Guildhall built in 1407, now a museum. The cathedral is one of the smallest in England. It has its origins in a religious establishment that was sacked by the Danes around 860, but it is noted for the carving of the canopies to the choir-stalls, the complete and well-preserved series of symbols of each month – a tradition thousands of years old – which can be found on the capitals, and the dramatic stained glass in the east window which dates from the fourteenth century.

The city's award-winning museum and art gallery is at Tullie House, a Jacobean residence in Castle Street; it has an exhibition on the railways of the town and area, as well as a herb garden, a display covering the Romans and an exciting audio-visual display on the border reivers. It is also the national study centre for the whole of Hadrian's Wall. Thanks largely to the bequest of the playwright and poet Gordon Bottomley, who died in 1948, the gallery includes works by Ford Maddox Brown, Edward Burne-Jones, Paul Nash, Samuel Palmer and Rossetti, as well as acquisitions of works by Lowry, Pissarro, Sickert and Stanley Spencer.

Index